EUROPEAN PERSPECTIVES

EUROPEAN PERSPECTIVES

ESSAYS

BY

ALEXANDER JACOB

LOGIC PUBLISHING

European Perspectives by Alexander Jacob
Editor: John Morgan
Cover Design: Andreas Nilsson

ISBN: 978-91-87339-65-3
©2020 Logik Förlag
Box 22120, 250 23 Helsingborg, Sweden
www.logik.se | www.freespeechlibrary.com
kontakt@logik.se

CONTENTS

I

German Socialism as an Alternative to Marxism: Werner Sombart and Oswald Spengler[1]

Today, when Marxism has come to be accepted as a legitimate political system, it would be salutary to revive the conservative reaction to this messianic doctrine evinced in the writings of German intellectuals at the turn of the twentieth century. While Marxism made steady inroads into the social structure of the German population through its high-sounding Hegelian dialectic and stirring slogans addressed to the working class, genuinely German minds were indeed horrified by the economic desiccation of social life that Marxism implied, and some of the German economists and social philosophers proposed social reforms of their own that were more naturally suited to the ethical and social constitution of the German people. Of these German alternatives to Marxism, I shall present here two versions: those of Werner Sombart, and Oswald Spengler. Of these, the former called his system German Socialism, and the latter Prussian Socialism. What is common to both these alternatives to Marxism is

---

[1] This essay was first published in *The Scorpion*, no. 21 (Winter 2000/2001), pp. 22-26.

that they consider Marxism as coincidental with the question of the Jewish involvement in European society.

I may briefly recall that Karl Marx (1818–1883) was born in an Orthodox Jewish family in the Rhineland and studied law, philosophy, and history at the universities of Bonn and Berlin. Marx began his career as a political economist in Paris through his association with the German, Friedrich Engels. His earliest economic work was the *Economic and Philosophic Manuscripts of 1844,* which reflected his absorption of Hegelianism, French socialism, and English economics. Expelled from France in 1845, Marx moved to Brussels, where he was brought into contact with the workers' movement, for which he drafted in 1848 the influential *Communist Manifesto.* This contained a critique of capitalism and a call for revolutionary socialism. During the 1848 revolutions, Marx was extradited from Brussels, and the remainder of his years were mostly spent in London, where he was financially supported by Engels, who had by now become an affluent industrialist. His major work produced in England was *Das Kapital* (1867), which remains the bible of Communism among Left-wing thinkers.

The complete rejection of philosophical discussion in *Das Kapital* crystallises the innate defect of the Jewish mind as much as Marx's exclusive focus on economic issues in his projects for the future society of man. Believing that capitalism was a transient stage in the evolution of society since it was based on the exploitation of labour by the capitalist minority which must sooner or later be swept aside by the masses, Marx outlined a coming anarchic utopia which would be entirely free of money, social classes, and even state-government. It may be noted that Marx himself was a professed anti-Semite, since he considered the Jews as predominantly capitalistic in spirit, but the social system that he propounded in its place was no less significative of the Jewish mentality than that of the capitalists he attacked. The cultural limitations of Marx's materialistic view of life, conditioned by what he called 'the mode of production of the material means of life', were therefore most clearly exposed by more genuinely philosophical German sociologists such as Sombart and Spengler.

Werner Sombart (1863–1941), the economist and social philosopher, is noted today for his several pioneering works on the capitalistic ethos. Although Sombart began his sociological career as a socialist in the Marxist vein, he gradually dissociated himself from the economical orientation of Marx's social theory in favour of a more voluntarist understanding of the springs of social evolution which supported the very patriarchal and aristocratic model of society which Marx had sought to destroy. In his *Die deutsche Volkswirtschaft im neunzehnten Jahrhundert* (The German National Economy in the Nineteenth Century, 1903), Sombart turned his back on the socialist glorification of progress which he saw as destructive to the human spirit and revived the medieval ideal of the guild community which involved, as Arthur Mitzman summarises it, 'the full absorption and development of the personality of the producer in his work; limited goals; and the shaping of the productive units on the model of the family community'.[2] The replacement of this original organic society by the artificial *Gesellschaft* (society), to use Ferdinand Tönnies' terminology, was consolidated by the Jew's interference in Germanic society. This was the case since the Jew is marked by abstract thought which is 'synonymous with indifference towards qualitative values, with the inability to appreciate the concrete, individual, personal, living'.[3] The symbolical expression of the Jewish capacity for abstraction is money, in which 'all the qualitative values of consumer goods are dissolved and appear only in quantitative determination'.[4] The proletariat, which is the typical social product of capitalism, is the element which suffers

---

[2] Arthur Mitzman, *Sociology and Estrangement: Three Sociologists of Imperial Germany* (New York: Alfred A. Knopf, 1973), p. 194.

[3] Werner Sombart, *Die deutsche Volkswirtschaft im neunzehnten Jahrhundert* (Berlin: Georg Bondi, 1903). Author's translation.

[4] *Ibid.*

most in the replacement of the patriarchal social ethos by the commercial, for 'every community of interest is dissolved, as also every community of labour' and 'bare payment is the only bond which ties the contracting parties together'.[5] The traditional comfort of religion, too, has been destroyed by capitalism, which typically bolstered the Liberal intellectual movements of the Enlightenment.

A further crucial difference between Sombart's developing German Socialism and Marxism is his distinction between the capitalist who is an entrepreneur and one who is a trader. Whereas Marx attempted to overcome the entrepreneur as a historically obsolete figure, Sombart championed the creative and organisational virtue of the entrepreneurial spirit against the merely rationalising and abstracting characteristics of the trader.[6] In Sombart's view, the entrepreneur thus becomes the economic representative of the typical Faustian spirit of the German hero, while the calculating trader is increasingly identified with the foreigner – particularly the Jews and the English.

In his war-time book, *Händler und Helden* (Traders and Heroes, 1915), Sombart discussed the sociological significance of the war between the English and the Germans in terms of the radical difference between the 'trader spirit' and the 'heroic spirit'. The trader aims at achieving mere 'happiness' through the negative virtues of 'temperance, contentedness, industry, sincerity, fairness, austerity . . . humility, patience,' etc., which will facilitate a 'peaceful cohabitation of traders'. The 'heroic spirit', by contrast, aims at fulfilling the mission of life as a task of the higher self-realisation of humanity through the positive, 'giving' virtues of 'the will to sacrifice, loyalty, guilelessness, reverence, bravery, piety, obedience, goodness', as well as the 'military virtues', for 'all

---

[5] Werner Sombart, *Das Proletariat: Bilder und Studien* (Frankfurt am Main: Rütten & Loening, 1906), p. 59. Author's translation.

[6] 'Der kapitalistische Unternehmer', in *Archiv für Sozialwissenschaft und Sozialpolitik*, no. 29 (1909), p. 729.

heroism first fully develops in war and through war'.[7] War for the English was a chiefly commercial enterprise, whereas for the German it was a defence of his soul from the deadening influence of this same commercial spirit.

However, already in his major works of the period – on *Die Juden und das Wirtschaftsleben* (The Jews and Economic Life, 1911) and *Der Bourgeois* (The Bourgeois, 1913) – Sombart had shown that the modern system of commercial capitalism was due not mainly to English Protestantism, as Max Weber had proclaimed in his *Protestantische Ethik und der Geist des Kapitalismus* (The Protestant Ethic and the Spirit of Capitalism, 1904–5), but to Judaism. In fact, Weber himself was forced, under the stimulus of Sombart's work, to distinguish between Protestant capitalism and the 'pariah capitalism' of the Jews, a distinction which corresponds to Sombart's own historical division of the development of capitalism into early and high capitalism. While Calvinism had been partially influential in the development of the commercial spirit in its rationalistic and legalistic philosophy, Sombart denied that Protestantism was synonymous with capitalism since, on the contrary, Lutheranism had at least encouraged a deepening of religious feeling among the Germans. Even other forms of Protestantism were marked by a generally anti-capitalistic spirit of niggardliness, and at most took over capitalistic forms from the existing economic life of the Catholics. The real source of the development of the high capitalistic stage of society is, however, the Jewish mind, according to Sombart – that which first introduced the chief characteristics of modern capitalism: namely, the unrestricted play of the profit motive through free-trade, usurious dealings, and ruthless business practices, especially with regard to non-Jews.

The identification of cheating in commercial transactions and the exploitation of other peoples as the chief causes of Jewry's financial power is most fully discussed by Sombart

---

[7] Werner Sombart, *Händler und Helden: Patriotische Besinnungen* (Munich: Duncker & Humblot, 1915), p. 65. Author's translation.

in *Die Juden und das Wirtschaftsleben*. Sombart locates the root of Jewish economics in the hereditary religion itself

> which in all its reasonings appeals to us as a creation of the intellect, a thing of thought and purpose projected into the world of organisms, mechanically and artfully wrought, destined to destroy and to conquer Nature's realm and to reign itself in her stead. Just so does Capitalism appear on the scene; like the Jewish religion, an alien element in the midst of the natural, created world; like it too something schemed and planned in the midst of teeming life.[8]

Capitalism indeed derives directly from the sheer profit-oriented usurious economic tradition of the Jews:

> modern capitalism is the child of money-lending – In money-lending all conception of quality vanishes and only the quantitative aspect matters – In money-lending economic activity as such has no meaning; it is no longer a question of exercising body or mind; it is all a question of success. Success, therefore, is the only thing that has a meaning. In money-lending the possibility is for the first time illustrated that you can earn without sweating; that you may get others to work for you without recourse to force.[9]

Sombart here points to the subtle form of commercial violence which constitutes the Jewish exploitative system. The Jews in general have disregarded the restraints on profit-making inherent in the traditional patterns of European economic life:

> [The Jew] paid no attention to the strict delimitation of one calling or of one handicraft from another, so universally insisted on by law and custom. Again and again we hear the cry that Jews did not content themselves with one kind of activity; they did whatever they could, and so disturbed the order of

---

[8] Werner Sombart, *The Jews and Modern Capitalism*, tr. M. Epstein (New York: E. P. Dutton & Co., 1913), p. 200.

[9] *Ibid.*, p. 186.

things which the guild system wished to see maintained.[10]

The alien status of the Jew *vis-à-vis* the host peoples among whom they lived served as a contributory factor to the success of their capitalistic endeavours, for their second-class status in society only spurred them on in their natural hatred and resentment of the host peoples whereby they took advantage of non-Jews under the sanction of their so-called religious laws:

> intercourse with strangers was bereft of all considerations, and commercial morality (if I may put it so) became elastic.[11]

The end result of the prevalence of the Jewish spirit in the West was the corruption of the very nature of Western man and society, for

> [b]efore capitalism could develop, the natural man had to be changed out of all recognition, and a rationalistically minded mechanism introduced in his stead. There had to be a transvaluation of all economic values.[12]

This ruinous transformation is effected basically through the resilient adaptation of the Jew to the society in which he resides. But this process of adaptation is an intellectually determined one and lacks the organic quality of true sympathy:

> That Lord Beaconsfield was a Conservative was due to some accident or other, or some political conjuncture; but Stein and Bismarck and Carlyle were Conservatives because they could not help it; it was in their blood.[13]

Indeed, the Jews lack sympathy for

---

[10] *Ibid.*, p. 140.

[11] *Ibid.*, p. 232.

[12] *Ibid.*, p. 227.

[13] *Ibid.*, p. 254.

every status where the nexus is a personal one. The Jew's whole being is opposed to all that is usually understood by chivalry, to all sentimentality, knight-errantry, feudalism, patriarchalism. Nor does he comprehend a social order based on relationships such as these. 'Estates of the realm' and craft organisations are a loathing to him. Politically he is an individualist – He is the born representative of the 'liberal' view of life in which there are no living men and women of flesh and blood with distinct personalities, but only citizens with rights and duties.[14]

The result is that the Jews themselves often do not seem to understand the real significance of the Jewish Question, and appear to think that the Jewish Question is only a political or religious one, believing that

> whatever can be neatly set down on paper and ordered aright by the aid of the intellect must of necessity be capable of proper settlement in actual life.[15]

With Sombart's understanding of the radical difference between the heroic Germanic spirit and the lowly Jewish commercial one, it is not surprising that he identified himself with the National Socialist movement during the first years of its regime, even though he later withdrew from active participation in its programmes. In his *Deutscher Sozialismus* (German Socialism, 1934), Sombart reinforces this difference between the two ethoses, pointing once again to the desire of the Marxist proletariat socialism for 'the greatest good of the greatest number'.[16] This utopian trait of the Marxists is evinced especially in their championing of modern industrialism, even though it wishes for a substitution of private economic organisation

---

[14] *Ibid.*, p. 247.

[15] *Ibid.*, p. 248.

[16] Werner Sombart, *A New Social Philosophy*, tr. K. F. Geiser (Princeton, NJ: Princeton University Press, 1937), p. 149.

with an economic-community organisation built on the social ownership of the means of production. The aim of social happiness is geared to the notion of 'liberty, equality, and fraternity' borrowed from the French Revolution, and betrays the same resentments that impelled the first European revolution. The methods used for its realisation are the reduction of the amount of physical labour that the proletariat is subjected to through the use of machines, and proper organisation involving the abolishment of the division of labour. The abolition of the centralisation of capital and the notion of private property will further enhance the prosperity of the masses. This dream of the communistic proletariat is bolstered by the idea of unending historical progress – not towards a higher mankind, but a 'happier' one. Simultaneously, all religious feelings of reverence before an other-worldly deity must be suppressed so that the people may rapidly achieve the dream of a this-worldly paradise which is, in fact, the real goal of the Jewish religion as well.

Unfortunately, this 'fatal belief in progress which ruled the ideal world of the proletarian Socialism even more than the world of Liberalism' is the chief cause of the inexorable decay of genuine human culture, for, as he says,

> to perpetually renew, hinders all culture – Only when in the course of history the traditions of belief, of morals, of education, and of organisation are dominant is it possible for a culture to unfold itself. For, in accordance with its very nature, culture is old, rooted, indigenous.[17]

The basis of all culture can be only the nation and not the state as such, for the nation is

> the political association in its endeavour to attain an end – The nation exists not because it lives in the consciousness of the individuals, but it exists as an idea in the realm of the spirit; it is 'spiritual individuality'.[18]

---

[17] *Ibid.*

[18] *Ibid.*, p. 162.

The people who constitute a nation are indeed an organism like the individual and possess the same origin, same historical destiny, and the same spiritual culture. It is on this cultural basis that one ought to distinguish the Jews as an alien nation. The Jews should be denied equal rights in holding leading and responsible positions, regardless of their spirit and character. He points with approval to the pre-Wilhelminian period, when

> the military corps and nearly the entire internal and judicial administration, with approved exceptions, were closed against the Jews. Had this practice been retained, and had the Jews been assigned to other important fields, such as the universities, law and other activities, the German fatherland and, by no means least, the Jews themselves, would have been spared heavy afflictions.[19]

The solution that Sombart suggests to the Jewish Question is the transformation of the institutional culture in such a way that 'it will no longer serve as a bulwark for the Jewish spirit' – that is, the 'spirit of this economic age' or of bourgeois society, so that Germans themselves no longer indulge in the alien ethos foisted on them by the Jews. The economic policy of the modern states must also be one directed in a corporative manner based on a system of estates, which will be free of the potential for exploitation in the Jewish system:

> self-interests are to be overcome and articulated in the state as a whole; nor, in such an order, does the individual find his place according to his own estimate, but receives the place assigned to him. That means the recognition of the primacy of politics. In other words, an order according to estates is not reconcilable with the principle of free enterprise and free competition. In a community in which capitalistic economy still rules, an estate system is a contradiction. Not until the state rests fundamentally upon institutions, that is, upon a legal order which imposes duties, can an estate-system fulfil its tasks.[20]

---

[19] *Ibid.*, p. 177.

[20] *Ibid.*, p. 204

The new legal order will be both hierarchical and embody a 'super-individual reason' directed at the welfare of the whole; this order will be fully represented by the state. Henceforth the domain of economics will be ruled by that of politics, focused essentially in its military virtue, while in the realm of economics itself, agriculture will occupy the first rank and business the last. The leadership of a strong or authoritarian socialist state must rest in one

> who receives his directions, not as an inferior from a superior leader, but only from God . . . He is not required to listen to the 'voice of the people', in so far as he does not recognise in it the voice of God, which can never speak from the accidental and changing totality of all citizens or indeed only from the majority of the citizens. The *volonté générale* which is to be realised is a metaphysical, not an empirical reality . . . The statesman serves no popular interest, but only the national idea.

Naturally, the leader will be supported in his national tasks by an elite of capable officials and autonomous public bodies.

Sombart's German Socialism is indeed quite indistinguishable from that of the Conservative Revolutionaries of the Weimar Republic such as Oswald Spengler, Arthur Moeller van den Bruck, or Edgar Julius Jung.[21] This should only confirm the much-neglected fact that what the anti-democratic and anti-liberal Germans were fundamentally fighting for in the Weimar Republic was the European ethos, as opposed to the Jewish, and that German socialism (as distinct from and irreconcilable with Marxist socialism) is as oriented toward the

---

[21] See Oswald Spengler, 'Prussianism and Socialism', in D. O. White (ed.), *Oswald Spengler: Selected Essays,* tr. D. O. White (Chicago: Henry Regnery Co., 1967); Arthur Moeller van den Bruck *Germany's Third Empire,* tr. E. O. Lorimer (London: Arktos, 2012); and Edgar Julius Jung, *Die Herrschaft der Minderwertigen = The Rule of the Inferiour,* 2 vols., tr. Alexander Jacob (Lewiston, NY: Edwin Mellen Press, 1995).

development of true moral culture and as hierarchically and neo-medievally organised as German conservatism.[22]

As representative of the Conservative Revolutionary position in the Weimar Republic, we may consider the political views of Oswald Spengler (1880–1936), whose social ideal is indeed termed 'Prussian Socialism' in his essay, '*Preussentum und Sozialismus*' ('Prussianism and Socialism', 1919). This essay was a sketch of the main themes of the second part of his two-volume magnum opus, *Der Untergang des Abendlandes* (The Decline of the West, 1918/1922). The burden of Spengler's argument in this essay is the difference between the so-called Marxist socialism which is based on alien, English and Jewish understandings of society and the genuine socialism of the Prussian state. The socialism of the English is demonstrated by Spengler to be a Viking-like individualism, which has encouraged the colonial rapacity of the British Empire and the mercantile ruthlessness of its leaders. The Norman conquest of England had put an end to the Anglo-Saxon way of life and introduced the 'piracy principle' whereby 'the barons exploited the land apportioned to them, and were in turn exploited by the duke'.[23] The modern English and American trade companies are enchained to the same motives of profiteering:

> Their aim is not to work steadily to raise the entire nation's standard of living, it is rather to produce private fortunes by the use of private capital, to overcome private competition, and to exploit the public through the use of advertising, price wars, control of the ratio of supply and demand.[24]

---

[22] See, for instance, the Introduction to my edition of Edgar Julius Jung's *Die Herrschaft der Minderwertigen*, *ibid*. For a brilliant modern statement of the genuine conservative position, as distinct from the conservative party programmes, see Roger Scruton, *The Meaning of Conservatism* (London: Macmillan, 1984).

[23] Oswald Spengler, 'Prussianism and Socialism', in *Selected Essays*, p. 62.

[24] *Ibid.*, p. 63.

The French democratic notions, on the other hand, are ruled by an anarchic love of pleasure, since what every individual in the French state wants is 'an equality of pleasure, equal opportunity for life as a pensioner'.

The Marxist doctrine, being a product of the Jewish mind, which is characterised by 'resentment', is based on envy of those who have wealth and privileges without work, and so it advocates revolt against those who possess these advantages. It is thus essentially a negative variant of the English ethos. It is not surprising, therefore, that the worker in the Marxist doctrine is encouraged to amass his own profits through private business, so that, as Spengler puts it, 'Marxism is' indeed 'the capitalism of the working class'. The Marxist system is thus the 'final chapter of a philosophy with roots in the English Revolution, whose biblical moods have remained dominant in English thought'.[25] In fact, as he goes on to say, 'a biblical interpretation of questionable business dealings can ease the conscience and greatly increase ambition and initiative'.[26] While the industrialists engage in commerce with 'money' as a commodity, the workers do the same with 'work'. In the Prussian state, on the other hand, work is not a commodity, but a 'duty towards the common interest, and there is no gradation – this is Prussian style democratisation – of ethical values among the various kinds of work'.

The Marxian solution to boundless private property is also a negative one: 'expropriation of the expropriators, robbery of the robbers'.[27] This is based on the 'English' view of capital, wherein

---

[25] *Ibid.*, p. 97. What Spengler does not explicitly observe here is that the biblical mode of thought which directed Puritan capitlistic industry is in fact a basically Jewish, voluntaristic one deriving from the conception of the universe as created by a Pantokrator who rules the creation with his Will as a personal Lord (see E. Zilsel, 'The Genesis of the Concept of Physical Law', in *Philosophical Review*, no. 51 [1942], p. 247ff). For a discussion of the Jewish origins of this concept as well, see Max Weber, *The Protestant Ethic and the Spirit of Capitalism,* tr. T. Parsons (London : George Allen & Unwin, 1930).

[26] 'Prussianism and Socialism', *loc. cit.*, p. 97.

[27] *Ibid.*, p. 118.

the billionaire demands absolute freedom to arrange world affairs by his private decisions, with no other ethical standard in mind than success. He beats down his opponents with credit and speculation as his weapons.

On the other hand, the Prussian sees property not as private booty, but as part of a common weal, 'not as a means of expression of personal power but as goods placed in trust, for the administration of which he, as a property owner, is responsible to the state'. Prussian socialism is thus essentially

> not concerned with nominal property, but rather with techniques of administration . . . The Old Prussian method was to legislate the formal structure of the total productive potential while guarding carefully the right to property and inheritance, and to allow so much freedom to personal talent, energy, initiative, and intellect as one might allow a skilled chess-player who had mastered all the rules of the game. This is largely how it was done with the old cartels and syndicates, and there is no reason why it could not be systematically extended to work habits, work evaluation, profit distribution, and the internal relationship between planners and executive personnel. Socialisation means the slow, decades-long transformation of the worker into an economic civil-servant, of the employer into a responsible administrative official with extensive powers of authority, and of property into a kind of old-style hereditary fief to which a certain number of rights and privileges are attached.[28]

The significance of the notion of the national state is completely ignored by Marx in his focus on 'society'. On the other hand, the Prussian form of socialism is based entirely on the notion of the primacy of the state, which is indeed the ideal of the Teutonic knight, diametrically opposed to the roving plunder of the Viking:

---

[28] *Ibid.*, p. 119f.

The Teutonic knights that settled and colonised the eastern borderlands of Germany in the Middle Ages had a genuine feeling for the authority of the state in economic matters, and later Prussians have inherited that feeling. The individual is informed of his economic obligations by Destiny, by God, by the state, or by his own talent . . . Rights and privileges of producing and consuming goods are equally distributed. The aim is not ever greater wealth of the individual or for every individual, but rather the flourishing of the totality.[29]

While English society is devoted to 'success' and wealth, the Prussian is devoted to work for a common national goal:

The Prussian style of living . . . has produced a profound rank-consciousness, a feeling of unity based on an ethos of work, not of leisure. It unites the members of each professional group – military, civil service, and labour – by infusing them with a pride of vocation, and dedicates them to activity that benefits all others, the totality, the state.[30]

The individual subsumed in the totality is, however, marked most strikingly by 'that glorious inner freedom, the *libertas oboedientiae* which has always distinguished the best exemplars of Prussian breeding.'[31] The administrative ideal that Spengler proposes for the Prussian state is, like Sombart's, corporative and hierarchical in structure:

Let us envision a unified nation in which every one is assigned his place according to his socialistic rank, his talent for voluntary self-discipline based on inner conviction, his organisational abilities, his work potential, consciousness, and energy, his intelligent willingness to serve the common cause. Let us plan for general work conscription, resulting in occupational guilds that will administrate and at the same time be guided by an administrative council, and not by a parliament.[32]

---

[29] *Ibid.*, p. 62.
[30] *Ibid.*, p. 47.
[31] *Ibid.*, p. 40.
[32] *Ibid.*, p. 88.

Parliamentarianism is not only inappropriate in a monarchical state such as the Prussian, but it is a tired and outmoded system which has lost the glory lent it by the 'gentlemen' and aristocrats who once ruled German and British politics. Now

> the institutions, the sense of tact and cautious observance of the amenities, are dying out with the old-style people of good breeding . . . The relationship between party leaders and party, between party and masses, will be tougher, more transparent, and more brazen. That is the beginning of Caesarism.[33]

Selfish individuals employ democratic forms of parliamentarianism to make the 'state' an executive organ of their own business interests, 'i.e. by paying for election campaigns and newspapers and thus controlling the opinion of voters and readers'.[34] Thus, democracy, in general is an unholy alliance of urban masses, cosmopolitan intellectuals, and finance capitalists. The masses themselves are manipulated by the latter two elements through their specific agencies: the press and the parties.[35] The intelligentsia represent 'abstract intelligence', not spiritual enlightenment, while the finance capitalists are supported by mobile fortunes distinct from the landed property of the true nobility. In fact, the League of Nations, the forerunner of our United Nations, was itself an instrument of big business, and was 'in reality a system of provinces and protectorates whose populations are being exploited by a business oligarchy with the aid of bribed parliaments and purchased laws'.[36]

As for the so-called 'internationalism' of modern Marxism, this is immediately recognised as a sham when one notes the diversity of races and of their responses to political movements.

---

[33] *Ibid.*, p. 89.

[34] *Ibid.*, p. 118.

[35] Oswald Spengler, *The Decline of the West*, tr. C. F. Atkinson (NY: Alfred A. Knopf, 1926), Vol. 2, p. 447; cf. Spengler, 'Prussianism and Socialism', *loc. cit.*, p. 75.

[36] Spengler, 'Prussianism and Socialism', *loc. cit.*, p. 118.

In fact, according to Spengler, the true 'International' is 'only possible as the victory of the idea of a single race over all the others, and not as the mixture of all separate opinions into one colourless mass'.[37]

The significance of Spengler's critique of English and Jewish ethics cannot be exaggerated, for it serves as a reminder of the importance of distinguishing between the English piracy principle and the German state idea, as well as between the false 'socialism' of Marx and its genuine Prussian form. The real meaning of socialism, according to Spengler, is

> that life is dominated not by a contrast of rich and poor but by rank as determined by achievement and ability. That is our kind of freedom: freedom from the economic capriciousness of the individual.[38]

Spengler, like Sombart, believed in the Prussian ideal of rule, not by popular parliamentary methods, but by an elite who would – like the military officer or bureaucrat – be characterised by devotion to duty and to the common good. As he declares, 'Authoritarian socialism is by definition monarchistic', for '[t]he most responsible position in this gigantic organism . . . must not be abandoned to ambitious privateers'. Although Spengler welcomed Hitler's movement as indicative of the revival of the 'disciplined will' of the Prussian spirit, he shied away from the question of Jewry and criticised the National Socialists for being too materialistic in their discussions of race. Also, in *Jahre der Entscheidung* (The Decisive Years, 1933), he indicated that he believed that the National Socialists had betrayed the Prussian elitism which he favoured by turning the revolution into a mass movement:

> the demagogue lives with the masses as one of themselves; the born ruler can use them, but he despises them.[39]

---

[37] *Ibid.*, p. 111.

[38] *Ibid.*, p. 130.

[39] Oswald Spengler, *The Hour of Decision*, tr. C. F. Atkinson (London:

However, Spengler seems rather unaware of the elitist character of Hitler's SS organisation and of its characterisation by precisely that 'war-like' quality which Spengler looked for in the rulers of the future ('armies, and not parties, are the future form of power'). Indeed, Spengler's view of nationalism, 'together with the monarchical idea latent in it',[40] as a transition to the Caesarism which he envisaged as the final outcome of the degeneracy of the modern age, may also be confirmed by the history of the National Socialist movement as a continuing battle for the establishment of the hegemony of the Germanic world-view against the Jewish one – whether capitalistic or communistic.[41]

We will have therefore noticed that the German socialism of the two thinkers considered here is essentially a moral Idea based on the strong-willed character of the Germanic race. Both thinkers, moreover, are united in their contempt for the Jew, whose chief modern political representative, Marx, is considered to be responsible for the perversion of the German feeling for social justice based on mutual co-operation into an unnatural warfare between the different classes of the same nation, for the ultimate benefit of an international organisation. Sombart's anti-Semitism is more exclusively economic and, for that reason, considers institutional reorganisation as sufficient for the elimination of the Jewish economic influence on society. Spengler's recognition of the irreconciliability of the Jewish ethos with the German on a spiritual level at the same time that he rejects racialism of the blood is a contradiction which leads him to believe that, once the Europeans and Americans have achieved a certain independent mastery of the new urban civilisation of the modern age, the Jewish financial expertise will become superfluous,

---

George Allen & Unwin, 1934), p. 202.

[40] *Ibid.*, p. 194.

[41] 'Marxism is the Capitalism of the Working Class' (Spengler, 'Prussianism, *loc. cit.*, p. 100).

causing the Jews as a force to reckon with to fade away. As he put it,

> To-day this Magian nation, with its ghetto and its religion, itself is in danger of disappearing – not because the metaphysics of the two Cultures come closer to one another (for that is impossible), but because the intellectualised upper stratum of each side is ceasing to be metaphysical at all . . . The lead that this nation has enjoyed from its long habituation to thinking in business terms becomes ever less and less (vis-a-vis the American, it has already almost gone), and with the loss of it will go the last potent means of keeping up a Consensus that has fallen regionally into parts.[42]

The social and political facts of the post-war world have proven Spengler tragically wrong in his underestimation of the pervasive and tenacious power of Jewry, both among its host nations and in its new home in the Middle East. This power is due precisely to the success that the Jewish mentality has had in eroding the metaphysical finesse of the European mind to the materialistic and rationalistic level of the former. The danger of Marxism is that, like the Jewish race from which it arose, it is virulently opposed to national cultures and to the natural, hierarchical, and autarkical ordering of European society. It is hardly surprising that these anti-nationalistic traits persist in European society today – if not under the guise of Communism as in the earlier part of this century, then under that of liberal democracy. Through the latter system, the Jews are thus able to continue – even more freely than in Communism – to foster intellectual and cultural corruption, as well as the consequent social dissatisfaction, in such a way as to benefit and perpetuate their own sterile commercial existence as an international power. The remedy to this problem, it must be realised sooner or later, lies in the reversion to more authentic versions of European socialism that are capable of countering the fragmenting tendencies of

---

[42] Spengler, *The Decline of the West*, Vol. 2, *ibid.*, p. 323.

Jewish rationalism and commercialism with the moral integrity and organic spiritual creativity that informed the cultural achievements of the Europeans, and that alone can ensure their survival in the future.

II

Erik von Kuehnelt-Leddihn and Julius Evola on the Bourgeoisie, Protestantism, and the *Protocols*[1]

Two books published in the early 1950s by two European aristocrats merit careful study by every contemporary European conservative since they express the authentic reactions of authentic noblemen to the revolutionary changes that Europe has suffered under the yoke of democracy and totalitarianism for so long. These are Erik, Ritter von Kuehnelt-Leddihn's *Liberty or Equality: The Challenge of our Time* (1952) and Baron Julius Evola's *Gli Uomini e le rovine* (Men Among the Ruins, 1953). Both Evola and Kuehnelt-Leddihn were opposed to democracy for its levelling tendencies, which they considered to be a mere transitional stage towards totalitarian systems – Communist as well as capitalist. However, while Kuehnelt-Leddihn focused on the democratic mania

---

[1] This essay was published as 'The Bourgeoisie, Protestantism, and the Protocols: The Anti-Democratic Thought of Erik, Ritter von Kuehnelt-Leddihn and Barone Giulio Cesare Evola' in *Counter-Currents*, December 31, 2014 (www.counter-currents.com/2014/12/kuehnelt-leddihn-and-evola/).

of equality – which he considered incompatible with liberty or true freedom – without clearly attributing this mania to the middle classes, Evola unequivocally identified the bourgeoisie and their innate mercantile nature – which militates against the warrior ethos of the earlier aristocratic societies – as the source of the evils of democracy.

Erik von Kuehnelt-Leddihn (1909–99) was, as a member of the Habsburg Empire's aristocracy, a monarchist and 'arch-liberal' in the tradition of Alexis de Tocqueville. He devoted his career mostly to championing the liberties that he felt were threatened by democratic and socialistic doctrines. Between 1937 and 1947 he lived and taught in America, returning there regularly after that time, from his native Austria, in order to lecture and continue his mission of improving American understanding of the mind and mentality of the Europeans. He was associated with the Acton Institute for the Study of Religion and Liberty and, before that, with the Ludwig von Mises Institute, from which the Acton Institute had branched off as a Christian offshoot. He was constantly aware of the difference between the Catholic monarchical order to which he belonged and the various democratic and totalitarian systems that sprouted all around him in post-1914 Europe, and his principal concern was to combat the levelling impulse of democracy which leads to the deprivation of liberties.

Already in 1943, during the war, he had written a work on political history called *The Menace of the Herd, or Procrustes at Large*[2] which discussed the defects of democracy and socialism in Europe, as well as in America and Russia. I shall restrict my observations mainly to the second of his political studies, *Liberty or Equality: The Challenge of our Time*,[3] and refer to the first only for contextual substantiation. The first part of *Liberty or Equality* is devoted to an examination of the

---

[2] Erik von Kuehnelt-Leddihn, *The Menace of the Herd, or Procrustes at Large* (Milwaukee, WI: Bruce Publishing Co., 1943).

[3] Erik von Kuehnelt-Leddihn, *Liberty or Equality: The Challenge of Our Time* (Caldwell, ID: The Caxton Printers, 1952).

inextricable connection between democracy and tyranny. In his earlier work, *The Menace of the Herd*, he had highlighted the connection between Europe's bourgeoisie and the development of capitalism. He pointed specially to the Protestant Reformation as that movement which liberated the capitalist spirit by strengthening the prestige of the usurious Jews in European society. The Protestant countries of northern Europe particularly developed with extraordinary speed into capitalist states, while the south lagged behind, possessing more traditional societies:

> [Jean Cauvin's] theocratic city state of Geneva had still a few aristocratic traits, but its soul was already essentially ochlocratic and bourgeois. At the time of his death we find a highly developed middle-class civilization and culture of a capitalistic and semirepublican character in the countries of the Rhine valley – in Switzerland, in the Palatinate, in Alsace, in Holland – but a similar process under the same accelerating influence can also be observed in districts further away: in southern France, in the British Isles, and in eastern Hungary.[4]

The problem of this new rule of money and technology was that, unlike the Catholic south, it was culturally sterile:

> Apart from a few poets we see these followers of Calvin contributing very little to the arts and letters. They lacked painters, musicians, architects of originality; hilarity was for them suspect and their humor was limited.[5]

There arose in the north also the dangerous slogan of 'progress':

> the old hierarchic and personal societies were hammered into shapeless masses by the two great products of "progress" – the megalopolis and the factory. "Progress" is *(a)* a collectivistic and *(b)* a purely urban ideal . . .[6]

---

[4] *Ibid.*, p. 51.

[5] *Ibid.*

[6] *Ibid.*, p. 58.

And hot on the heels of this new-fangled idea of 'progress' came the notion of "humanity":

> "Humanity" as such scarcely existed as a living principle in the Middle Ages because man had in regard to eternity no collective existence. Individuals sacrificed themselves for their families, their manorial lords, kings, cities, rights, privileges, religion, their beloved Church or the woman they loved, in fact, for everything or anybody to which or to whom they had a *personal* relationship. The anonymous sand-heap "humanity" was unknown to medieval man and even the concept of the "nation" was not equivalent to a gray mass of unilingual citizens but was looked upon as a hierarchy of complicated structure . . . The collective singular "humanity" was only created after the Reformation as a living unit.[7]

The bourgeoisie responsible for capitalism and democracy, however, were not in sympathy with the lower classes, which were more closely allied with the aristocracy:

> The capitalistic bourgeoisie of the nineteenth century (mainly if we consider the upper-middle classes) stood for an election system which excluded the lower classes even from indirect influence in the government. The middle-class "democrat" frequently dreads the manual laborer, who often sided with the aristocrat, and he usually hates the peasant politically, partly on account of the ingrained loathing of the agrarian elements against the city, partly on account of the conservative-patriarchal structure and tendencies of the farming population.[8]

Thus, the will-o'-the-wisp of 'humanity' rendered men not more 'fraternal', but less:

---

[7] *Ibid.*, p. 58f.

[8] *Ibid.*, p. 56f.

Democratistic culture and civilization lowered them to the unhierarchic sand heap but, paradoxically, did not bring them any nearer to each other. The thought of a common creator and a common origin can alone unite human beings . . .[9]

This is indeed the source of the alienation of modern democracies:

> In the hierarchic Tyrol, people are much nearer to each other than in "democratic" New York, and even the Albanian practising his vendetta is more good neighborly than the inhabitant of modern Berlin or Stockholm.[10]

Interestingly, Kuehnelt-Leddihn traces the beginnings of popular democracy, or 'ochlocracy', to the materialistic thought of Jean Cauvin and the denial of the next world by the Enlightenment thinkers who ushered in the French Revolution:

> There is little doubt that atheism, agnosticism, and the denial of the other world are partially   responsible for the rapid technical development which gave us, apart from exquisite instruments for mass destruction, various means to bridge time and space.[11]

Mass distribution of commodities through technology makes everything available to everyone because '[n]obody should have the right to pride himself on being the sole possessor of a specific thing', and the sociological result is a rapid collectivisation:

> "Democracy" in its first stages is intrinsically a struggle against privileges and later democratism continues this bitter, depersonalizing struggle against everybody and anybody with the help of the demoniacal magic of technique.[12]

---

[9] *Ibid.*, p. 59.
[10] *Ibid.*, p. 60.
[11] *Ibid.*, p. 35.
[12] *Ibid.*, p. 65.

Universal education, too, is identified by Kuehnelt-Leddihn as one of the 'collectivist' features of democracy:

> instead of sticking to the hierarchic principle in the most aristocratic of all domains – intellectual education – a whole corollary of compromises with the mass spirit were made in this field; education became thus finally nothing but another factor of leveling applanation side by side with industrialism.[13]

It is significant also that the middle classes were especially opposed to the Catholic Church on account of its hierarchical nature and its preoccupation with mysteries, which in a democracy had to be rationalised by the half-educated masses. As he notes,

> [i]t must also be kept in mind that the class most antagonistic to the Church has been during the past centuries the middle class, or the bourgeoisie. It is the middle class in France, Austria, Germany, Bohemia, and Moravia which shows the greatest percentage of Protestants . . .[14]

Unlike Evola, Kuehnelt-Leddihn does not consider liberalism as a distinguishing characteristic of democracy but, rather, he considers democracy's characteristic obsession to be the desire for equality, which as mentioned above contradicts the natural desire for liberty. Freedom itself he defines in *Liberty or Equality* as the liberty to develop one's personality:

> the greatest amount of self-determination which in a given situation is feasible, reasonable and possible. As a means to safeguarding man's happiness and protecting his personality it is an intermediary end, and thus forms part of the common good. It is obvious that under these circumstances it cannot be brutally sacrificed to the demands of absolute efficiency nor to efforts towards a maximum of material welfare.[15]

---

[13] *Ibid.*, p. 66.

[14] *Ibid.*, p. 69.

[15] *Ibid.*, p. 2.

In this context, he takes particular care to distinguish Anglo-Saxon democracy from Continental, for the former is traditionally directed from above and retains the character of an 'aristocratic republic',[16] whereas the latter tends to mass democracy, which leads to totalitarianism. He also reminds us that:

> some of the best minds in Europe (and in America) were haunted by the fear that there were forces, principles and tendencies in democracy which were, either in their very nature or, at least, in their dialectic potentialities, inimical to many basic human ideals – freedom being one among them.[17]

The principal defects of democracy derive from its materialistic concerns, and thus its mass production, militarism, ethnic nationalism, racialism, and all tendencies toward 'simplification' that tend towards uniformity and sameness, what he calls 'identitarianism'. He quotes Lord Acton's remark that '[l]iberty was the watchword of the middle class, equality of the lower'. This is, however, different from his own statement in *The Menace of the Herd* that '[l]iberty is the ideal of aristocracy, just as *equality* stands for the bourgeoisie and *fraternity* for the peasantry'.[18] Indeed, if equality were the prime demand of the lower classes, as Lord Acton had suggested, the levelling that Kuehnelt-Leddihn points to is clearly not due to them but rather to elites that organise them as 'masses of men who are "alike and equal" attracted by small and vulgar pleasures'. His quotation from Alexis de Tocqueville in *Liberty or Equality* indeed makes this quite clear:

> above this race of men stands an immense and tutelary power, which takes upon itself alone to secure their gratifications, and to watch over their fate. That power is absolute, minute, regular, provident and mild. It would be like the authority of a parent, if, like that authority, its object was to prepare men

---

[16] *Ibid.*, p. 135.

[17] *Ibid.*, p. 14.

[18] *Ibid.*, p. 48.

for manhood; but it seeks, on the contrary, to keep them in perpetual childhood: it is well content that the people should rejoice, provided they think of nothing but rejoicing. For their happiness such a government willingly labours, but it chooses to be the sole agent and arbiter of that happiness: it provides for their security, foresees and supplies their necessities, facilitates their pleasures, manages their principal concerns, directs their industry, regulates the descent of property, and subdivides their inheritances – what remains but to spare them all the care of thinking and all the trouble of living?[19]

We see from this description of the workings of democracy that the latter is a maternalistic caricature of the paternalistic political ideal that we shall see is propounded by Evola. Even though Kuehnelt-Leddihn does not, like Evola, blame the bourgeoisie for this forced levelling of the lower classes, he does notice that capitalist mass production and nationalistic militarism are creations of the bourgeois capitalists rather than of the proletariat.

We may note also that he considers racial nationalism as a form of 'proletarianism' where whole nations are elevated to pseudo-aristocratic status.[20] However, it may be inferred from his own discussion of the different attitudes to nationalism and racialism among Catholics and Protestants (see below) that this nationalism and racialism are not so much characteristics of the lower classes as of those who exploit the democratic system, which must be principally the capitalist middle classes.

In general, Kuehnelt-Leddihn does not accentuate the dangerous revolutions of the bourgeoise in monarchical or aristocratic states, nor their baneful effect on the lower classes, for which it has little sympathy. He does not also clearly relate the Jews in European society to the transformations from monarchies to democracies and collectivist societies that European countries have undergone in recent history, although he cursorily hints at the Old Testament roots of the materialism and obscurantism that mark Protestant democracies. His main concern being the

---

[19] *Ibid.*, p. 29.

[20] *Ibid.*, p. 58.

defence of individual and social liberty, he studies the gradual transformation of democratic governments into tyrannies. If in democratic states actual dictators do not emerge on the scene, totalitarianism manifests itself nevertheless in the bureaucratic apparatus of the state, which caters to the social welfare needs of the lower classes. Here again he is – on the surface, at least – rather lenient towards the middle classes, and does not seem to consider that a benevolent state bureaucracy might cater to the genuine needs of the people while it may also interfere in the financial ambitions of the middle classes.

In the development of democracy into totalitarian tyranny, Kuehnelt-Leddihn rightly notices the crucial role played by Protestantism. Unlike Evola, who does not discuss the nature or dangers of Protestantism in his critique of modern Catholicism, Kuehnelt-Leddihn squarely places the blame for democratic degeneration on Protestantism. He notes that, ideologically, democracies depend on relativist principles which are themselves characteristic of the Protestant movements:

> relativism, which the clear thinker and logician rejects, plays an enormous role in the political and spiritual realm of democracy. We leave it to the psychologist to determine the feminine implications of such relativism. But relativism and readiness for compromise go hand in hand, and an absolute refusal to compromise on fundamentals (a Catholic rather than a Protestant trait) would soon bring democratic machinery to a standstill.[21]

While Catholics are unpliable when it comes to dogma, Protestants are rather more subjective in their approach to doctrinal matters. Catholics are consequently more convinced of their principles and do not favour latitudinarianism. As he notes,

> Catholic dogma, except for an "increase in volume," has remained unchanged, and commentary on it has varied only within certain limits. Protestantism, on the other hand, is

---

[21] *Ibid.*, p. 126.

in a constant process of evolution. Whereas the faith of Catholics can be exposed to the process of *diminuation de la foi* ("diminution of the faith"), that of the Protestant is also subject to the *rétrêcissement de la foi* ("narrowing of the faith").[22]

On the other hand, Protestantism is a more fanatical religion that insists, in a mediaevalist and Old Testament manner, on God alone, while Catholicism has always considered God and Man with equal care. This explains the wonderful artistic explosion of the Renaissance and the Baroque, which are relatively poorly represented in Protestant lands:

> Thus the key to the real understanding of the Catholic cultures of the European Continent and of South and Central America is, for the Protestant as well as for the Catholic of the British Isles and North America, an understanding and appreciation of the cultural, artistic and intellectual values of Humanism, the Renaissance and the Baroque.[23]

The Protestant insistence that 'religion is a private matter' is completely opposed to the Church's concern with the 'totality of human culture',[24] culture itself being distinguished from civilisation, which caters to the merely material comforts of mankind:

> Yet while civilization is basically lack of friction, smoothness, comfort, and material enjoyment we have to look at traditional Christianity – with its violent opposition to euthanasia, abortion, contraception, pacifism, and individualism – as being something "uncomfortable."[25]

---

[22] *Ibid.*, p. 180.

[23] *Ibid.*, p. 182.

[24] *Ibid.*, p. 39.

[25] *Ibid.*, p. 36f.

Protestantism and Calvinism also posses an Old Testament tendency to take earthly success as a sign of divine favour[26] which is absent in Catholic nations, 'where the beggar is a "useful" member of society and commercialism is not highly appreciated'. Protestants fearful of social fragmentation naturally tend to the lowest common denominator that mark collectivist systems. Catholics, on the other hand, are more personally developed than the Protestants, who through their proneness to compromise, solidarity, cooperation, and neighbourliness[27] tend to be more conformist than Catholics, and even more bigoted. In fact, one of the distinguishing features of democracy itself – for Kuehnelt-Leddihn as well as for Evola – is that it is 'anti-personalistic' and 'collectivistic',[28] and its tendency to exert 'horizontal pressure' results in totalitarian systems.

It is not surprising thus that 'Calvin established in Geneva the first truly totalitarian police-state in Europe'.[29] The French Revolution, too, was of Protestant inspiration:

> It is also obvious that the ideological substance of the French Revolution is almost in its entirety the product of Protestant dialectics. Although there are some minor Cartesian and Jansenistic elements in the political philosophy of '89 and '92, the main impulses came from America, Britain, Holland and Switzerland.[30]

This is why also, as Kuehnelt-Leddihn reminds us, 'Count Keyserling calls America *socialistic* in a deeper sense and arrives at the conclusion that 'most Americans want to obey as no soldiers have ever done'.

---

[26] This is, of course, typical of the land of the Puritans, America. The transformation of Hebrew-inspired Puritanism into finance capitalism in America has been well-noted by Werner Sombart in *Die Juden und das Wirtschaftsleben* (1911). See also Chapter V, below.

[27] *Ibid.*, p. 192.

[28] *Ibid.*, p. 134.

[29] *Ibid.*, p. 183.

[30] *Ibid.*, p. 187.

Catholics, by contrast, are undemocratic by nature:

> it is virtually certain that the Catholic nations, with their love for personal liberty, their earthly pessimism, their pride and scepticism, will never in their hearts accept parliamentary democracy.[31]

Catholic countries deprived of monarchy tend to bureaucraticism, anarchy, or party-dictatorships rather than to democracy:

> We have to ask ourselves whether in the most extreme cases, when violent temperament is combined with thorough ideological incompatibility (Spain, Portugal, Greece, South America), government from above on a bureaucratic basis is not the only safeguard against the alternative of anarchy and party dictatorship (125)

Catholicism is essentially paternalistic and hierarchical, qualities that Evola too prescribes for his organic conservative state. Catholics favour patriarchs but not policeman; they can even often be anarchists and militate against the state. While the uniformity of the ruling political parties in Protestant countries facilitates nationalism as well as totalitarianism, Catholics are not popular nationalists, nor do they favour centralisation, but rather federalism.[32] Kuehnelt-Leddihn gives the example of the Geman federalist Constantin Frantz (1817--91), who opposed centralised totalitarian regimes – and he reminds us that the Prussians, too, were not pan-Germanic but rather dynastic.

The political solution to the inherent problems of democratic government that is propounded by Kuehelt-Leddhin is a hereditary monarchy with local organs of self-government. Unlike dictators, monarchs are restricted by Christian law, and here the doctrine of human imperfection – or 'original sin' – serves as a moderating influence in monarchies as well as it

---

[31] *Ibid.*, p. 207.

[32] *Ibid.*, p. 201.

does in democracies. Monarchy, like Catholicism, is paternalistic and not 'fraternal'. The reason that such a parternalistic rule – typical also of Catholic orders – is superior is that it obliges the ruler to be more responsible than democratically-elected leaders are. Monarchies are not oligarchical, plutocratic, or prone to corruption, since money does not rule the state as in democracies. Further, the monarch not only represents political responsibility, but also fosters 'great' statesmen within his government possessed of a comparable commitment to the duties of a state. A monarchy is also more efficient with its bureaucracy than is a democracy, and more capable of undertaking grand ventures.

Monarchs are in most cases biologically superior, and hereditary rule constitutes an organic rule which is contrary to variable party rule. They are trained for rule from childhood, and have a moral and spiritual education for their office. At the same time, they have greater respect for subjects[33] and protect minorities, since they do not depend on any majority support. Monarchies also tend to be international and ethnically mixed, thus serving as a unifying force.[34]

As democracies depend on what the Jewish socialist historian Harold Laski called a 'common framework of reference'[35] or consensus, there is in fact less freedom of expression in democracies than in monarchical states. This is particularly true of Catholic states, which are marked by different levels of enlightenment and thereby do not fall into the trap of Protestant utopianism. Catholicism does not believe that all are capable of the same education and understanding, since it is constantly conscious of the notion of human imperfection, or 'original sin'. The liberality of the Catholic in general arises from generosity, and not from relativistic reasoning that forcibly reconciles opposites.

Unfortunately, the greater liberties enjoyed in traditional Catholic monarchies have been curtailed in recent times by

---

[33] *Ibid.*, p. 152.

[34] See also *ibid.*, p. 159.

[35] *Ibid.*, p. 97.

Protestant regimes. But Kuehelt-Leddihn reminds us that only thirteen percent of the European continent's population are followers of Protestant creeds.[36] And it should be borne in mind turnip

> that the countries of continental Europe all need a mission, a final end, a metaphysical goal – which even elections, increased exports, more calories and better dental care are not going to obviate.[37]

It is therefore of vital importance that one must 'strive to help the European continent find its own soul'.[38] Following Kuehnelt-Leddihn's discussion of monarchism and Catholicism and their natural opposition to republicanism and Protestantism, we may assume that what is needed is a restoration – insofar as it is possible – of the Catholic monarchical system:

> 'Only thus can the Continent hope to become again what it used to be, a *tierra libre y real* – a Free and Royal Land'.[39]

* * *

The political tenets of the Sicilian nobleman Julius Evola (1898–1974) have been somewhat obscured by his 'traditionalist' interests in esoteric systems such as Hermeticism, Zen Buddhism, and yoga.[40] People have a general notion that he was a sympathiser of both the Italian Fascist and the German National Socialist movements, but a closer reading of his later works –

---

[36] *Ibid.*, p. 205.

[37] *Ibid.*, p. 207.

[38] *Ibid.*, p. 208.

[39] *Ibid.*

[40] The only detailed study of Evola's political thought to date is Paul Furlong's *Social and Political Thought of Julius Evola* (London: Routledge, 2011).

especially his major political work, *Men among the Ruins*[41] – will reveal that he was closer to the Fascist ideology, especially as represented by the philosopher Giovanni Gentile, than to the racialist thinkers of the National Socialist Reich such as Alfred Rosenberg or Walther Darré.

More forcefully than Kuehnelt-Leddihn, Evola identifies the bourgeoisie as the source of the problems of the modern world, since they are the chief representatives of the doctrines of Liberalism based on the primacy of the individual. Liberalism is a materialistic and utilitarian philosophy insofar as it takes into consideration only the material needs of the individuals that constitute society. Its feigned campaigns of liberty are belied by the fact that exploitative capitalism is a natural result of bourgeois materialism:

> The turning point was the advent of a view of life that, instead of keeping human needs within natural limits in view of what is truly worthy of pursuit, adopted as its highest ideal an artificial increase and multiplication of human needs and the necessary means to satisfy them, in total disregard for the growing slavery this would inexorably constitute for the individual and the collective whole.[42]

The individualism fostered by Liberalism results in an atomism and fragmentation of society that is then countered by forms of totalitarianism which are equally inadequate in their merely quantitative and economic concerns. Totalitarianism is, according to Evola, order imposed from above on a formless people. Marx was indeed right in attacking the bourgeoisie, but erred seriously in forcing the proletariat to serve as the cornerstone of a utopian society that is characterised by sterile uniformity:

> Totalitarianism, in order to assert itself, imposes uniformity.

---

[41] Julius Evola, *Men among the Ruins*, tr. Guido Stucco (Rochester, VT: Inner Traditions, 2002).

[42] *Ibid.*, p. 173.

In the final analysis, totalitarianism rests and relies on the inorganic world of quantity to which individualistic disintegration has led, and not on the world of quality and of personality.[43]

Thus, totalitarianism destroys all the vestiges of organic development that previous bourgeois states may have retained from their aristocratic past:

Totalitarianism, though it reacts against individualism and social atomism, brings a final end to the devastation of what may still survive in a society from the previous "organic" phase: quality; articulated forms, castes and classes, the values of personality, true freedom, daring and responsible initiative, and heroic feats.[44]

The exaltation of the 'worker' in socialist as well as collectivist systems is also a universalisation of the essentially servile nature of liberalist economic thought.

The solution to the problems inherent in any bourgeois ordering of society consists in the development of personality rather than individualism among the people. Among nations, too, autarky should be encouraged rather than the internationalism of global commerce:

It is better to renounce the allure of improving general social and economic conditions and to adopt a regime of austerity than to become enslaved to foreign interests or to become caught up in world processes of reckless economic hegemony and productivity that are destined to sweep away those who have set them in motion.[45]

The necessary control of the economy can be undertaken only by the state. The class conflicts focused on by Marx should be corrected by a corporative system, or a system of estates such as in the Middle Ages:

---

[43] *Ibid.*, pp. 151-52.

[44] *Ibid.*, p. 151.

[45] *Ibid.*, p. 176.

The fundamental spirit of corporativism was that of a community of work and productive solidarity, based on the principles of competence, qualification, and natural hierarchy, with the overall system characterized by a style of active impersonality, selflessness, and dignity.[46]

Of prime importance in the corporative system of earlier European history is the fact that

The usury of "liquid assets" – the equivalent of what today is the banking and financial employment of capital – was regarded as a Jewish business, far from affecting the whole system.[47]

In other words, Jewish usury was, if utilised by states, always regarded as a feature of outcasts of European society.

Evola's solution to capitalism's social injustice focusses on the elimination of the parasitical capitalists and the deproletariatisation of the workers:

the basic conditions for the restoration of normal conditions are, on the one hand, the deproletarization of the worker and, on the other hand, the elimination of the worst type of capitalist, who is a parasitical recipient of profits and dividends and who remains extraneous to the productive process.[48]

Unlike Marx, who sought to turn the proletariat into owners and directors of companies, Evola maintains that the proper eradication of the evils of capitalism should begin with the curtailment of the rampant profit-motivation of the companies and their directors by the state. All companies should therefore, in general, be responsible to the state.[49] All national

---

[46] *Ibid.*, p. 225.

[47] *Ibid.*, p. 225.

[48] *Ibid.*, p. 226.

[49] *Ibid.*, p. 231.

economic issues should be dealt with in the Lower House of parliaments, while the Upper House should be the sole representative of the political life of the nation. The latter body cannot be an elected one, but must be appointed – and for life.

In fact, this Upper House should act as what Evola calls the ruling elite, or 'Order', of a nation. He would like to see the core of this Order to be constituted of members of the old aristocracies who are 'still standing . . . who are valuable not only because of the name they carry, but also because of who they are, because of their personality'.[50] Aiding this core would be a class of warriors, who are naturally not the same as soldiers, who are merely paid military employees. Warriors are ruled by concepts of honour and loyalty to the nation, such as were found recently in the Prussian military echelons, and the strict subordination of the mercantile class to this warrior class is an essential feature of Evola's political doctrine.

For the state is indeed essentially a masculine socio-political phenomenon, in contrast to society, which is mainly feminine. The state formed by *Männerbünde*, or male ruling elites,

> is defined through hierarchical, heroic, ideal, anti-hedonistic, and, to a degree, even anti-eudemonistic values that set it apart from the order of naturalistic and vegetative life.[51]

The reason for the exclusive position of ruling males in a state is that

> every true political unity appears as the embodiment of an *idea* and a power, thus distinguishing itself from every form of naturalistic association or "natural right," and also from every societal aggregation determined by mere social, economic, biological, utilitarian, or eudemonistic factors.[52]

This power is sacred in its origins, as it was for example in the

---

[50] *Ibid.*, p. 284.

[51] *Ibid.*, p. 124.

[52] *Ibid.*, p. 122.

concept of *imperium* in the Roman Empire, for it expresses a transcendent order, a concept that will be familiar to students of the Fascist philosopher, Giovanni Gentile.[53]

Democracy and socialism signal a dangerous shift from the rule of the masculine state to that of the feminine society and the *demos*; a state is not a 'nation', either, since a nation is typically a motherland, even if it is occasionally called a fatherland in some countries. The Romans, Franks, as well as the Arabs who spread Islam, were all constituted of *Männerbünde* at first, and only when they degenerated into democracies did they become 'nations'.

Since any conservative revolution needs to restore the primacy of the warrior ethos, it must begin by opposing the mercantile one of the bourgeoisie:

> the "conservative" idea to be defended must not only have no connection with the class that has replaced the fallen aristocracy and exclusively has the character of a mere economic class (i.e., the capitalist bourgeoisie)—but it must also be resolutely opposed to it. What needs to be "preserved" and defended in a "revolutionary fashion" is the general view of life and of the State that, being based on higher values and interests, definitely transcends the economic plane, and thus everything that can be defined in terms of economic classes.[54]

This would also require the formation of a new elite, or Order:

> The essential task ahead requires formulating an adequate doctrine, upholding principles that have been thoroughly studied, and, beginning from these, giving birth to an Order. This elite, differentiating itself on a plane that is defined in terms of spiritual virility, decisiveness, and impersonality, and where every naturalistic bond loses its power and value, will be the bearer of a new principle of a higher authority and sovereignty; it will be able to denounce subversion and demagogy in whatever form they appear and reverse the downward

---

[53] See Chapter V, below.

[54] *Ibid.*, p. 114.

spiral of the top-level cadres and the irresistible rise to power of the masses. From this elite, as if from a seed, a political organism and an integrated nation will emerge, enjoying the same dignity as the nations created by the great European political tradition. Anything short of this amounts only to a quagmire, dilletantism, irrealism, and obliquity.[55]

Disregarding the norms of a socialistic state, the organic conservative state must be a 'heroic' one that is not based on the family nucleus, but on the *Männerbünde* which produce the leaders of the state. These men will even abjure a family life for a dedication to the task of ruling:

> As far as a revolutionary-conservative movement is concerned, there is a need for men who are free from these bourgeois feelings. These men, by adopting an attitude of militant and absolute commitment, should be ready for anything and almost feel that creating a family is a "betrayal"; these men should live *sine impedimentis,* without any ties or limits to their freedom. In the past there were secular Orders where celibacy was the rule . . . the ideal of a "warrior society" obviously cannot be the petit-bourgeois and parochial ideal of "home and children"; on the contrary, I believe that in the personal domain the right to an ample degree of sexual freedom for these men should be acknowledged, against moralism, social conformism, and "heroism in slippers."[56]

There is no danger of the line of rulers' extinction, even though they may follow a celibate life, since

> the example of those centuries-old religious orders that embraced celibacy suggests that a continuity may be ensured with means other than physical procreation. Besides those who should be available as shock troops, it would certainly be auspicious to form a second group that would ensure the hereditary continuity of a chosen and protected elite, as the

---

[55] *Ibid.*, p. 132.

[56] *Ibid.*, p. 271.

counterpart of the transmission of a political-spiritual tradition and worldview: ancient nobility was an example of this.[57]

The organic conservative state will be based not on individuals, but on persons, whose *raison d'être* is their personality and its higher development. This realisation of the personality of an individual is equivalent to his freedom. The 'free' person is indeed free of the claims of his lower nature and demands a complete self-mastery. The most highly developed or differentiated person is the absolute person, or leader:

> The "absolute person" is obviously the opposite of the individual. The atomic, unqualified, socialized, or standardized unity to which the individual corresponds is opposed in the absolute person by the actual synthesis of the fundamental possibilities and by the full control of the powers inherent in the idea of man (in the limiting case), or of a man of a given race (in a more relative, specialized, and historical domain): that is, by an extreme individuation that corresponds to a de-individualization and to a certain universalization of the types corresponding to it. Thus, this is the disposition required to embody pure authority, to assume the symbol and the power of sovereignty, or the form from above, namely the *imperium*.[58]

Thus, unlike Kuehnelt-Leddihn, who championed hereditary monarchy, Evola seems to favour an enlightened dictator, or one who belongs to a new aristocratic order of men.

The state formed by this elite will be not only organic, but also hierarchical, and firmly based on the principle of authority.[59] In fact, this principle is the core of any organic state, which must necessarily grow from a definite centre:

---

[57] *Ibid.*

[58] *Ibid.*, p. 140.

[59] We may remember in this connection the typical Jewish aversion to authoritarian states and personalities in Theodor Adorno's *The Authoritarian Personality* (1950).

A State is organic when it has a center, and this center is an idea that shapes the various domains of life in an efficacious way; it is organic when it ignores the division and the autonomization of the particular and when, by virtue of a system of hierarchical participation, every part within its relative autonomy performs its own function and enjoys an intimate connection with the whole. In an organic State we can speak of a "whole" – namely, something integral and spiritually unitary that articulates and unfolds itself – rather than a sum of elements within an aggregate, characterized by a disorderly clash of interests. The States that developed in the geographical areas of the great civilizations (whether they were empires, monarchies, aristocratic republics, or city-states) at their peak were almost without exception of this type. A central idea, a symbol of sovereignty with a corresponding, positive principle of authority was their foundation and animating force.[60]

The basis of all authority is itself a 'transcendent' quality, as Gentile had also insisted:

Conversely, the organic view presupposes something "transcendent" or "from above" as the basis of authority and command, without which there would automatically be no immaterial and substantial connections of the parts with the center; no inner order of single freedoms; no immanence of a general law that guides and sustains people without coercing them; and no supra-individual disposition of the particular, without which every decentralization and articulation would eventually pose a danger for the unity of the whole system.[61]

Only an organic state can absorb all the manifold differences and conflicts that may exist within a state:

Even contrasts and antitheses had their part in the economy of the whole; as they did not have the character of disorderly

---

[60] *Ibid.*, p. 149.

[61] *Ibid.*, p. 153.

parts, they did not question the super-ordained unity of the organism, but rather acted as a dynamic and vivifying factor. Even the "opposition" of the early British parliamentary system was able to reflect a similar meaning (it was called "His Majesty's most loyal opposition"), though it disappeared in the later party-ruled parliamentary regime.[62]

Nationalism, too, should be avoided if it is of the popular sort rather than one based on the concept of a spiritual nation:

In the first case, nationalism has a leveling and antiaristocratic function; it is like the prelude to a wider leveling, the common denominator of which is no longer the nation, but rather the International. In the second case, the idea of the nation may serve as the foundation for a new recovery and an important first reaction against the internationalist dissolution; it upholds a principle   of differentiation that still needs to be further carried through toward an articulation and hierarchy within every single people.[63]

His vision of a regenerated Europe is one of an organic, sacred empire, or *imperium,* centred not on 'the concepts of fatherland and nation (or ethnic group)' which 'belong to an essentially naturalistic or 'physical' plane', but on 'a feeling of higher order, qualitatively very different from the nationalistic feeling rooted in other strata of the human being':[64]

The scheme of an empire in a true and organic sense (which must clearly be distinguished from every imperialism, a phenomenon that should be regarded as a deplorable extension of nationalism) was previously displayed in the European medieval world, which safeguarded the principles of both unity and multiplicity. In this world, individual States have the character of partial organic units, gravitating around *a unum quod non est pars* (a one that is

[62] *Ibid.*, p. 149.

[63] *Ibid.*, p. 249.

[64] *Ibid.*, p. 276.

not a part, to use Dante's expression) –namely, a principle of unity, authority, and sovereignty of a different nature from that which is proper to each particular State. But the principle of the Empire can have such a dignity only by transcending the political sphere in the strict sense, founding and legitimizing itself with an idea, a tradition, and a power that is also spiritual.[65]

The chief hurdles to the formation of a new Europe are American cultural hegemony, the yoke of democratic government, and 'the deep crisis of the authority principle and the idea of the State'.[66] But even though the task of unifying Europe may be a formidable one, it must be attempted, with the planning and organisation undertaken from the top down by the new elite 'Orders' of the various nations that constitute it.[67]

As regards the religious foundations of a state or empire, Evola is remarkably pessimistic in his estimation of the power of Catholicism to provide these, since he considers it to be excessively committed today to a liberal democratic path which has deprived it of its traditional political force. In fact, he considers the anti-Ghibelline or Guelfian movement of the Middle Ages to be the very source of the secularisation of the modern state. Thus, it would be better

to travel an autonomous way, abandoning the Church to her destiny, considering her actual inability to bestow an official consecration on a true, great, traditional and super-traditional Right . . .[68]

In spite of his callous treatment of the Catholic Church and its potential as the religious basis for a conservative state, Evola does examine in greater detail the subversive effects of another international sect, Judaism, whose political ambitions were

---

[65] *Ibid.*, p. 277.

[66] *Ibid.*, p. 285.

[67] *Ibid.*, p. 278.

[68] *Ibid.*, p. 215.

exposed in the so-called *Protocols of the Learned Elders of Zion,* (1903) which, even if not based on fact, would represent a literary depiction of the totalitarian goals of the Jews.[69] As Evola explains:

> the only important and essential point is the following: this writing is part of a group of texts that in various ways (more or less fantastic and at times even fictional) have expressed the feeling that the disorder of recent times is not accidental, since it corresponds to a plan, the phases and fundamental instruments of which are accurately described in the *Protocols*.[70]

The principal evil of the international Jews' design is their thorough economisation of modern life:

> the economization of life, especially in the context of an industry that develops at the expense of agriculture, and a wealth that is concentrated on liquid capital and finance, proceeds from a secret design. The phalanx of the modern "economists" followed this design, just as those who spread a demoralizing literature attack spiritual and ethical values and scorn every principle of authority.[71]

Not only was Marxism a useful tool of the Jews, but also those biological and philosophcal doctrines that fostered atheism, such as Darwin's evolutionary biology and Nietzsche's nihilism. The Jews further employ various tactics of subversion, having recourse to counterfeit doctrines of so-called 'traditionalism' and 'neo-spiritualism':

> The content of this "traditionalism" consists of habits, routines, surviving residues and vestiges of what once was, without a real understanding of the spiritual world and of what

---

[69] Indeed, the *Protocols* should be classified with Aldous Huxley's *Brave New World* (1932) and George Orwell's *Nineteen Eighty-Four* (1949) as fictive non-fiction.

[70] *Ibid.*, p. 240.

[71] *Ibid.*

51

in them is not merely factual but has a character of perennial value.[72]

The effect on the individual of these various subversive movements is

> to remove the support of spiritual and traditional values from the human personality, knowing that when this is accomplished it is not difficult to turn man into a passive instrument of the secret front's direct forces and influences.[73]

The most efficacious way of combating the subversion of international Judaism or Zionism is for the new warriors to learn to operate on the metaphysical plane, maintaining an 'unconditioned loyalty to an idea', since that is 'the only possible protection from occult war; where such loyalty falls short and where the contingent goals of 'real politics' are obeyed, the front of resistance is already undermined'. As he warns those who wish to undertake a conservative revolution or counter-revolution,

> no fighter or leader on the front of counter-subversion and Tradition can be regarded as mature and fit for his tasks before developing the faculty to perceive this world of subterranean causes, so that he can face the enemy on the proper ground. We should recall the myth of the Learned Elders of the *Protocols:* compared to them, men who see only "facts" are like dumb animals. There is little hope that anything may be saved when among the leaders of a new movement there are no men capable of integrating the material struggle with a secret and inexorable knowledge, one that is not at the service of dark forces but stands instead on the side of the luminous principle of traditional spirituality.[74]

***

---

[72] *Ibid.*, p. 245.

[73] *Ibid.*, p. 241.

[74] *Ibid.*, p. 251.

We see, therefore, that unlike Kuehnelt-Leddihn, Evola focuses on the bourgeoisie as the chief source of the democratic degeneration of modern Europe, just as his discussion of the 'occult' dimensions of the ongoing subversion helps one to concentrate on international Jewry as the principal agents of subversion that must be combated in a counter-revolution. Unfortunately, Evola does not place much hope on either a hereditary monarchy or Catholicism as the twin foundations of traditional European society, but instead seeks to build a new knightly Order that will yield strong, enlightened leaders for the European states.

The lack of enthusiasm for Catholicism in Evola's discussion of the state is, however, corrected by Kuehnelt-Leddihn's perceptive analysis of the difference between Catholicism and Protestantism. In strong contrast to Evola's negative attitude toward the modern Church, Kuehnelt-Leddihn's account of political history places a marked emphasis on established religion, and especially on Catholicism, in his formulation of the conservative state. Any contemporary attempt to return Europe to its natural pre-democratic vitality may therefore have to start not only from Evola's warnings of the dangers of the mercantile bourgeoisie and of the surreptitious war of the Jews against the European aristocratic traditions, but also from Kuehnelt-Leddihn's revelations regarding the deleterious effects that the relativist and materialist temper of Protestantism has had on modern European society.

III

Two Aesthetic Critiques of Capitalism:
Theodor Adorno and Hans-Jürgen Syberberg[1]

In a world marked by financial gangsterism in the West (as well as in Russia), violent sectarian conflicts in the Middle East, and expanding economic ambitions in China, the question of the preservation of the European tradition may seem at first glance to be an intellectual extravagance. But with the increasing uncertainties facing us in the future, our past may be the greatest source of strength left to us. Anybody who has studied the history and art of Europe will realise that its cultural development has for two millennia been intimately related to the monarchical rule of the continent as well as to the religious support of this rule by, first, the Indo-European religions of Greece and Rome, and then Christianity. The concept of an atheist proletarian state projected in the nineteenth century by the Jewish political economist Karl Marx, and realised in the twentieth by the Soviet Union as well as America, the two

---

[1] This essay was first presented as a talk at the *Revolt against Civilisation* conference, organised in Denmark in May 2011.

powers that divided Europe between themselves after the war, was indeed the wrecking ball that demolished the authentic Europe. In its place was substituted the sterile economic regimentations of the present European Union. Both the Communist and American colonisations of Europe were of course made possible by the debacle that Germany suffered at the end of the Second World War. With the fall of Communism as well twenty years ago, virtually the whole of Europe is now under the American sphere of influence. Unfortunately, the Jewish-American rulers will not – much less even than the Russian Communist ones – allow Europe to recover its own life and character because of their fear of the anti-Semitism that was part of the last German effort to reorganise the continent in an independently European way.

Since the task of protecting Europe from the socio-cultural devastations of Marxism, either Communist or capitalist, is one that was already attempted by the Germans before and during the war, it would be useful to learn from the German understanding and experience of this problem. It is for this reason that I should like to discuss the cultural and political commentary on Germany during and after the war that is contained in an important book written thirty years ago by the German film director Hans-Jürgen Syberberg: *Vom Unglück und Glück der deutschen Kunst nach dem letzten Kriege* (On the Misfortune and Good Fortune of Art in Germany after the Last War).[2] This is indeed a unique work of modern German social history whose political and cultural insights express the authentic genuine German spirit as few other artistic works of post-war Germany have. In a century dominated by various varieties of Marxist ideology, in the Soviet Union as well as in the capitalist West (where its Trotskyist internationalist

---

[2] Hans-Jürgen Syberberg, *Vom Unglück und Glück der deutschen Kunst nach dem letzten Kriege* (Munich: Matthes & Seitz, 1990). English edition: tr. Alexander Jacob, *On the Fortunes and Misfortunes of Art in Post-War Germany* (London: Arktos, 2017).

agenda is now disguised as 'Neo-conservatism'),[3] it is inspiring to read the views of a genuinely German thinker whose mind was formed by a traditional, rural Prussian upbringing and the idealistic thought characteristic of German Romanticism, although it is true that Syberberg is also sympathetic to certain Jewish socialist thinkers of the early part of the twentieth century such as Hans Mayer, Ernst Simon Bloch, and Hannah Arendt,[4] whom he considers as being more allied to the authentically German intellectual tradition than the thinkers and artists who established themselves in Germany after the war.

The numerous ruminations which constitute Syberberg's work delve, evocatively and hauntingly, not only into the author's own past in Pomerania during and after the Second World War but also into the harrowing past of his country, which he rightly considers as having suffered its first mortal blow with Prussia's defeat in 1918. For the Prussian Reich had represented the acme of the organised German social ethos, and the defeat of Adolf Hitler's grandiose ambitions for a thousand-year Reich in 1945 made it even more difficult to recover this ethos, since it allowed the Americans to erase all memory of the real Germany and radically reconstruct the western part of the country under their control in their own plastic image.

In the last part of the work, written amidst the fall of the

---

[3] The Neoconservative movement in America, headed by people like Irving Kristol (one of whose articles was entitled 'Memoirs of a Trotskyist', *The New York Times Magazine*, January 23, 1977) and Norman Podhoretz, includes many former Trotskyist Communists who moved from 'the Left' to 'the Right' when they detected strains of nationalism in the Stalinist Soviet Union, as well as anti-Semitism among American negroes during the Civil Rights Movement of the sixties. Their adoption of 'conservatism' as their political banner was designed to divest classical Conservatism of its inherent national-cultural tendencies and to transform the Jewish leaders of what Max Weber had (in the 1920 edition of his *The Protestant Ethic and the Spirit of Capitalism*) called 'pariah capitalism' into a new proletarian 'elite'.

[4] See Syberberg's Preface to my English edition of this work, *On the Fortunes and Misfortunes of Art in Post-War Germany*.

Berlin Wall, Syberberg grasps at what then appeared as a possibility for the regeneration of the unified country through the unspoiled social spirit of the Germans from the East. Unfortunately, these hopes have by now been largely disappointed, since the easterners, upon being freed from their Communist chains, were only too eager to plunge into the capitalist trough. As a result, there was little chance of the capitalist westerners themselves learning anything of the virtues of austerity from those from the East who may have remained untainted or unhurt by Marxism. Nevertheless, despite the present subjection of the modern world to Jewish-American socio-political dictates,[5] Syberberg's book serves to remind its readers – be they German, American, or otherwise – of the basic falseness of the self-proclaimed success of the Americans *vis-à-vis* the lands that they have brought under their control through brute force and social indoctrination. The latter has taken the form either of deliberate re-education, as in post-war Germany, or of incessant media propaganda, as in the rest of Europe. Reading Syberberg's views on the hollow state of present-day German culture, in spite of its much-vaunted post-war 'economic miracle', allows us to recognise the devastating effect of the Jewish-American socio-political ideology on any genuine culture that it may come into contact with or seek to dominate.

The real tragedy of the Second World War is thus seen, in retrospect, to have been not only the enormous numbers of dead, injured, and displaced that it produced, but also the almost total extinction of the art that Germany had supported and attempted to maintain through the centuries as the highest significance of the political life of the nation and its empire. With the total collapse of Germany at the end of the Third Reich, the centre of European culture, what Syberberg calls its 'backbone', was indeed broken. And in this work, Syberberg achieves what he calls

---

[5] For the preponderant influence of Jewish 'cultural Marxist' thinkers on modern American society, see Kevin B. Macdonald's *The Culture of Critique: An Evolutionary Analysis of Jewish Involvement in Twentieth Century Intellectual and Political Movements* (Westport, CT: Praeger, 1988).

a *Trauerarbeit* (work of mourning), which he considers essential for the recovery of the damaged German psyche. Germany had for too long been forbidden to grieve for its own losses while the Jews, on the other hand, have been allowed to commemorate the massacre of their people as a turning point in world history. I may briefly mention here that Syberberg was born in 1935 in Nossendorf, Pomerania to a Prussian ruling class family. He lived in Rostock and Berlin until 1945, and then moved to West Germany in 1953, where he did his doctorate on Friedrich Dürrenmatt at the University of Munich. Influenced also by Bertolt Brecht's anti-realistic 'epic theatre', Syberberg began producing documentary films in 1963, but did not achieve international fame until his film on the Bavarian king Ludwig II, *Ludwig: Requiem für einen jungfräulichen König* (Ludwig, Requiem for a Virgin King, 1972), which combined Brechtian dramatic tableaux with a Wagnerian soundtrack to great evocative effect. This was followed by *Karl May* in 1974, about the romantic German novelist who wrote of adventures among exotic peoples like the Indians of America and the Turks of the Ottoman Empire, and whose novels were admired by Hitler. In the following year Syberberg filmed a long interview with Winifred Wagner, the wife of Richard Wagner's son Siegfried, called *Winifred Wagner und die Geschichte des Hauses Wahnfried von 1914-1975* (Winifred Wagner and the History of the Wahnfried House, 1977). His next film was on Hitler himself and called *Hitler. Ein Film aus Deutschland* (Hitler: A Film from Germany, 1977). This was followed by a film of Wagner's *Parsifal* in 1981. His final films were cinematic versions of monologue dramas featuring Edith Clever, such as *Die Nacht* (The Night, 1984), *Penthesilea* (1987), *Die Marquise von O* (The Marquise of O, 1989), *Ein Traum, was sonst?* (A Dream, What Else?, 1994) – which evoked the end of the Bismarckian Reich – and a two-part film called *Höhle der Erinnerung* (Cave of Memory, 1997).

Apart from directing films, Syberberg also published books about film-making and social and cultural history starting with *Syberbergs Filmbuch* (Syberberg's Film Book, 1976), *Die freudlose Gesellschaft. Notizen aus dem letzten Jahr* (The Joyless

Society: Notes from Last Year, 1981), *Der Wald steht schwarz und schweiget* (The Forest is Black and Silent, 1984), the present work in 1990, and *Der verlorene Auftrag. Ein Essay* (The Lost Job: An Essay, 1994). Perhaps the most important of these is the work I have chosen to discuss, and it is also one of the most controversial. Soon after its publication, Hellmuth Karasek remarked hysterically in *Der Spiegel* that 'one remembers that it is with such sentences, such thoughts, such hollow conspiracy theories that the book-burning of 1933 and the Final Solution of 1942 were prepared and made possible . . . They are not abstruse babble, they are criminal'.[6] Oppressed by the controversy that arose around the book, Syberberg gradually withdrew from the film world, deciding to retire to his parental house in Nossendorf, which was his original artistic nursery.

Although the Jewish attacks on Syberberg were expectedly vicious, many of the criticisms of American consumer society in his work had already been made during the Second World War by the Jewish Marxist thinker Theodor Adorno (né Wiesengrund, 1903–1969) in his *Dialektik der Aufklärung* (Dialectic of Enlightenment, 1944). Adorno, along with Max Horkheimer, founded the Frankfurt School in Germany, and later moved to America, where he lived between 1938 and 1949. Adorno's critique of capitalism took the form of a Marxist analysis of liberal consumerism in the West, especially America, and gives evidence of the fact that even the European Marxists were rather more developed in their artistic sensibilities than the capitalist Americans. In the *Dialektik der Aufklärung*, Adorno revealed the failure of the Enlightenment to liberate human beings from fear and to install them as masters.[7] Instead, capitalism had continued its ethos of 'domination' in a threefold manner, including domination by human beings, domination of the nature of

---

[6] 'Mit solchen Sätzen, mit solchen Gedanken, mit solchen dumpfen Verschwörungstheorien ist, man erinnere sich, die Bücherverbrennung von 1933, ist die "Endlösung" von 1942 vorbereitet und ermöglicht worden . . . Sie sind kein abstruses Geschwätz, sie sind verbrecherisch'.

[7] This is, of course, the goal of Marxism as well.

human beings, and the domination of some human beings by others. This domination is a proof of the 'unfree' character of modern society since it is bent on the neutralisation or destruction of the 'other' in its pursuit of 'progress'.[8] Adorno's critique of capitalist consumer society in the fourth chapter of this work, 'The Culture Industry: Enlightenment as Mass-Deception', is largely the same as Syberberg's, since it points to a totalitarian system of production wherein

> [t]he unified standard of value consists in the level of conspicuous production, the amount of investment put on show. The budgeted differences of value in the culture industry have nothing to do with actual differences, with the meaning of the product itself.[9]

Culture considered as an industry can only produce repetitions of the same based on formulas which leave no scope for the imagination. The constant pressure to produce new effects (what is today called 'innovation') is accompanied by the insistence to conform to the old successful patterns and conventions of cultural production. Thus, the goal of the culture industry is 'obedience to the social hierarchy', and '[a]nyone who resists can survive only by being incorporated'.[10] The totalitarian effect of capitalist society is clear from the fact that 'freedom to choose an ideology, which always reflects economic coercion, everywhere proves to be freedom to be the same'.[11]

At the same time, the free availability of so-called 'art' in the capitalistic society also makes it relatively worthless, so that '[in] the culture industry respect is vanishing along with criticism:

---

[8] This explains why the German world-view was especially targeted after the war as an intolerable obstacle to the continuance of capitalist domination.

[9] Theodor Adorno & Max Horkheimer, *Dialectic of Enlightenment: Philosophical Fragments*, tr. Edmund Jephcott (Stanford: Stanford University Press, 2002), p. 97.

[10] *Ibid.*, p. 103f.

[11] *Ibid.*, p. 136.

the latter gives way to mechanical expertise, the former to the forgetful cult of celebrities'.[12] Ultimately, the consumer himself becomes cynical:

> Reduced to mere adjuncts, the degraded works of art are secretly rejected by their happy recipients along with the junk the medium has made them resemble. The public should rejoice that there is so much to see and hear.[13]

Adorno proclaimed that his aim in this work was to effect a 'dialectical enlightenment of the Enlightenment' whereby, by understanding the origin and goal of thought itself, thought would overcome the current dominations through reconciliation. However, given Adorno's pessimistic view of the possibility of correcting capitalistic society, it is hard to see how any transformation of society could be possible. In fact, Adorno does not even seem to wish for such a transformation, even through art, for he believes that art is 'the social antithesis of society'[14] and, following Marx, cannot be detached from its present social context. Thus, at most, an artwork can simultaneously challenge the way things are and suggest how things could be better, but practically, it leaves things unchanged. In other words, Adorno's aesthetics, unlike the idealistic, gives art no independence for the execution of its vital ethical role as a regenerator of society.

Worse, Adorno's postwar 'critiques' are informed by a perverse Jewish revanchism which is most clearly revealed in his *Philosophie der neuen Musik* (*Philosophy of Modern Music*, 1949), where, in his eulogy for Arnold Schoenberg's atonal music, he outlines what he considers to be the purpose of all modern music:

> What radical music perceives is the untransfigured suffering of man . . . The seismographic registration of traumatic shock

---

[12] *Ibid.*, p. 130.

[13] *Ibid.*

[14] Theodor Adorno, *Aesthetic Theory*, tr. Robert Hullot-Kentor (London-New York: Continuum, 1997), p. 8.

becomes, at the same time, the technical structural law of music. It forbids conformity and development. . . . Modern music seeks absolute oblivion as its goal. It is the surviving message of despair from the shipwrecked.[15]

We see that Adorno's real aim here is to seek revenge on the Germans by imposing the sense of total despair felt by the Jews after the Third Reich upon the entire European folk among whom they still lived. In fact, Adorno is well-known for his infamous remark that 'Nach Auschwitz kein Gedicht mehr' ('to write a poem after Auschwitz is barbaric').[16] In other words, the horrible discordance of modern music and art is the only art that he as a Jew would permit the Europeans, lest they become barbaric in their cultural elevation once again.

In his 1955 essay, 'The Aging of the New Music',[17] Adorno himself criticised the modern music which he had fostered for what he called its 'abstract negation', but he nevertheless refused to welcome harmony again. Adorno had sought to drive German aesthetics in diverse contradictory directions so that it would have nothing more to do with fascism. Having in this way wrought the complete destruction of music, especially in Germany, Adorno honestly commented in his *Aesthetic Theory* that 'it is thinkable . . . that great music . . . was possible only during a limited phase of humanity'.[18] What he failed to add, however, is that this phase – which really came to an end at the turn of the century, but continued to live a fitful life until the Second World War – was a pre-Schoenbergian one marked by a relative absence of Jewish participation and interference in its musical creativity. We see that Adorno, for all his European cultural background, is finally as cynical as the other Marxist-anarchists who attacked

---

[15] Theodor Adorno, *Philosophy of Modern Music*, tr. A. G. Mitchell and W. V. Blomster (New York: The Seabury Press, 1973), p.41f.

[16] Theodor Adorno, *Prisms*, tr. Samuel & Shierry Weber (Cambridge, MA: The MIT Press, 1955), p. 34.

[17] In Theodor Adorno, *Essays on Music*, tr. Susan H. Gillespie (Berkeley, Los Angeles: University of California Press, 2002).

[18] Adorno, *Aesthetic Theory*, p. 8.

classical European art as part of the anti-bourgeois, anti-nationalist, anti-imperialist Russian Revolution.

What is to be borne in mind regarding the so-called modernist world is that it is not really a 'free' one but one that has been programmed, at a very deep psychological level, by a long process of indoctrination that began in the forties with Adorno himself, even though Adorno's own critique of capitalism had been based on his Marxist recognition of its lack of freedom. In the late forties, Adorno co-directed the anti-dictatorial 'Authoritarian Personality' project, which prepared the way for the 'drug/rock/sex' counterculture that became a reality two decades later. In 1950, Adorno and his colleague Max Horkheimer were recalled to Germany by the so-called 'Congress for Cultural Freedom', funded by the CIA, to de-Nazify the post-war German educational system and cultural institutions. In the fifties, modern art and music were therefore strenuously promoted by the Congress in Europe as well as in America.

The Jewish programme of indoctrination naturally had a serious damaging effect on that German culture which had been at the heart of European civilisation for hundreds of years. This devastation is what Syberberg laments in his work. Syberberg's description of the anti-natural and inaesthetic forms that modern art assumes begins with a critique of the Enlightenment social standards that still control it:

> The Enlightenment analysis of social sciences signifies an attack on monarchist history and the old orders of life and the world itself, and a colonisation of these human domains through the democratic imperialism of self-destruction.[19]

The commercially driven art of today is entirely opposed to Nature: 'All sensibilities, knowledge, instinct, and powers of imitation are withered, debauched, ridiculed, both of the landscape and of the soul and the feelings'. The result of the democracy propagated by the French Revolution and its Marxist-socialist pupils is 'to make oneself rich, to suppress the great and high

---

[19] All translations from Syberberg's book are the author's.

and destroy the individual for a quick and cheap trial of throw-away society, for a pollution of Nature, until the latter strikes back'.

We have noted already from Adorno's aesthetic analyses the essential similarity between the collectivist ethos of Communism and that of capitalism, both of which seek only material happiness and do not respect the natural foundations of art, which grows from the culture of a land, and – almost literally – from its soil. According to Syberberg, art is virtually impossible without a nationalistic and aristocratic social system, since democratic forms will always cater to the material welfare of the majority of people regardless of their origin and not to their spiritual elevation, which can only arise from the complete education of an individual within the social and religious orders of his own culture. This is necessarily rooted in his own land, and cannot spring from the atheistic internationalism of Marxist societies, whether Communist or capitalist.

The reason why art finds it so difficult to return to its source in Nature is that true art indeed has to be based on 'blood and soil'. It is an art that does not want power or money. But in Germany, after the war, the natural springs of art were forbidden owing to their associations with Hitler's 'blood and soil' doctrines. The paranoid aversion to Hitler initiated by the Jews has indeed resulted in three taboos in the realm of art: the first, the prohibition of beauty, since Hitler's Reich was considered as an 'aestheticisation of politics'; second, the prohibition of all high art by Adorno in his remark that 'to write a poem after Auschwitz is barbaric'; and third, the rejection of agrarian culture as being closely linked to Hitler's 'blood and soil' mythos. We see clearly the impossibility of true art in a world that removes from it all its genuine bases.

The result of this unnatural perversion of European aesthetics is the unrelenting preference of contemporary art for

the small, the low, the crippled, the sick and dirty over brightness, of the base as a strategy from below . . .

And culture in general is at the same time ossified into a museum industry wherein

> [o]ur democracy affords art in super houses with a tax budget, according to scientifically explained knowledge, cultivates old handicrafts as the last bastion of dying skills, and . . . counts success according to the number of entry-tickets sold.

The highest value of this post-Hitlerian aesthetics is

> the pluralistic postulate of freedom and the equality of styles, orientation, and individuals . . . Through the loss of co-ordinates everything becomes equal.

As a result, as Adorno had already pointed out, the art of the modern age is always monotonous. As Syberberg puts it: 'Art of always similar texts and scores, where nothing can change but the fashions of directorial style. The triumph of an art for the museum cannot be greater'. Thus, the collapse in the East is answered by the weariness in the West which may be evinced 'in the book fairs and film festivals, and on the stages and in the art exhibitions – the collapse of architecture as a culture-ordering factor of Nature'.

The worst aspect of this modern cultural industry is its ostracisation of those who do not subscribe to its rules. This is done either through open battle or through silencing. In fact, in postwar Germany, 'a mafia system associated with living the lie of democracy' had come to power:

> an unholy alliance of a Jewish Leftist aesthetics against the guilty to the point of boredom and lies crippling all cultural life, so that guilt was able to become an imagination-killing business, no longer fruitful but restricting, as the criterion of production and of the public . . . Anyone who went with the Jews or with the Leftists made a career, and it certainly did not have anything to do with love or understanding or, indeed, inclination.

Syberberg is convinced (rightly, as we have seen) that Adorno and the other founding fathers of the post-war Germany had deliberately fostered an art that would result in 'the crippling of the superior race':

> the race of superior men [*Herrenmenschen*] has been seduced; the land of poets and thinkers has become the fat booty of corruption, business, and lazy comfort.

In film, the technologically most advanced art of the age, Hollywood 'sells its interpretations of world-understanding in dress code, seductive gestures, action, and facial overtures between enticement and intimidation to the youth of the world, interpreting anew the world histories, like a revenge on the world . . .' Especially in Germany, memory has turned into a business of the victors, representing themselves as victims of the Holocaust in films and TV serials, while the Germans must be forever represented as a guilty people who must never lament their own losses:

> The children were turned to hatred against their fathers, and art became a case of neurosis as a sign of the suppression. Everybody was enticed with wealth, intimidated with guilt, brought up to be grateful, and the significance of thought and life was threatened and all values changed . . .

But 'death without a purificatory lament promotes the memory-business, with those enticed able to be blackmailed to their own self-exploitation . . .' And

> [o]ne who does not escape from his memories without activating them becomes sick and, with a corresponding demand, wicked to the point of self-destruction. And it is a rejection of the knowledge that there must always be art overcoming here through the beauty of love, like the conception of a new and different world.

We note here the difference between Syberberg's championing of art as a redemptive influence on society and Adorno's use of it as an instrument of revenge. And we realise that all of post-war aesthetics has indeed constituted a Jewish strategy of social control and power, whether it at first called itself proletarian or whether it now calls itself liberal or Neo-conservative.

Indeed, the principal phenomenon of the history of the twentieth century may be considered to have been the triumph of the Jewish god over the Christian-European. As Syberberg puts it: 'Two thousand years in their mission to subject the world to themselves, the Oriental god mingled with Greek, Roman, and North-European peoples. A god who made them powerful and great, and brought them their end'. But eventually, 'The era which began with Christ, the distant god from the East, ended with Hitler's death; Jerusalem conquers, finally for all, through the others for us'. The result of the loss of Prussia and Germany was that Israel quickly gained in international political, social, and cultural power, and

> the Jewish interpretation of the world followed upon the Christian, just as the Christian one followed Roman and Greek culture. So now Jewish analyses, images, definitions of art, science, sociology, literature, politics, the information media – dominate. Marx and Freud are the pillars that mark the road from East to West. Neither are imaginable without Judaism. Their systems are defined by it. The axis USA-Israel guarantees the parameters. That is the way people think now, the way they feel, act, and disseminate information. We live in the Jewish epoch of European cultural history. And we can only wait, at the pinnacle of our technological power, for our last judgement at the edge of the precipice . . .

Of the major themes of modern European history, Syberberg considers the most crucial to have been, first, the disappearance of Prussia and the partition of Germany after the war into capitalist and Communist countries, the former re-educated and seduced by material prosperity and the latter violated with totalitarian force; second, Auschwitz and the exodus of the European Jews to Israel and America; and third, the expulsion of Germans directly after the war from East to West Germany. Syberberg's analysis of the decay of European culture thus concentrates on the destruction of Prussia at the end of the First World War and the acceleration of Germany's downfall in the Third Reich. Syberberg even considers Hitler to have been a 'stranger' from Austria[20] who appeared on the German political scene only to oversee the end of Prussia. And he appeared thus only through the inglorious means of democracy.

In the third part of the book, which was written on the occasion of the fall of the Berlin Wall, Syberberg expresses his amazement at the turn of events during the bloodless revolution of that year. He also wonders whether Germany may, through its reunification, be revived through the infusion of fresh, unspoiled blood from the East, or whether the eastern Germans would sink all too readily into the Americanised commercial morass of the West.

The fall of Communism in 1989 seemed at first glance to usher in the possibility of a renewed cultivation of the European spirit under the reunification of East and West Germany:

> The peoples awaken not from Stalinism, but from Marxism as from the darkest nightmare, and Europe is once again one . . . . The lie of rational socialism is exposed . . . And all the neurotic art which was based on it, and all the Left's intellectual systems will not be anymore what they were.

Syberberg thus rightly considers Marxism (and not Stalinism, as the Jews would have us think) as one of the greatest evils that Europe suffered after the French Revolution. He hopes for a new system

> [w]here the states are founded anew according to the new law of freedom, which is not unlimited under the influence of manipulated opinions, but free, where being free means free of the pressure of intimidation and false enticements. And

---

[20] Syberberg, as a champion of the Prussian state, tends to discount the great contributions of the Habsburgs to Europe's cultural development.

where democracy is not the expression of the majority, where equality does not always have to be right, but which should be represented by the necessary minority of the higher level of quality – as art, as a model, may demonstrate.

However, he is already aware that the West's present intelligentsia is incapable of any artistic regeneration: 'How can anything like freedom ever come from these men of books, of the arts, the theatre and films, or music, when they were the first victims of the re-education . . .' Rather, '[r]escue can come only from below, from the uncontaminated and the poorest, from the East'. Thus, everything depends on the extent to which the newly liberated men from the East resist the degeneracy of the West:

> It will all depend on how far the eastern part of Europe will have the strength to defy the western dangers, to resist many enticements, basically . . . Perhaps the East will awaken to a new awareness of a clever symbiosis, and the West has – at the right moment – the right people to bring back those things that were driven away to a happy union . . .

The Marxist destruction of Prussia was accompanied in the western part of Germany by American promises of 'democracy and peace as alternatives to Prussia'. What it led to, however, was 'manifest corruption in the West and . . . bankruptcy in the East'. Particularly, the 'industrialisation of agriculture in the West [corresponded] to that of the forced collectivisation in the East', so that the agrarian basis of German culture was completely destroyed. Thus, the Marxist and capitalist schemes have together sought to destroy the vitality of Germany, and 'the catastrophe of Germany was only a step on the way to the world'.

The Marxist systems imposed on Germany by the Communist side, as well as from the capitalist, are indeed alien forms which Germany cannot continue to live with:

> For what was once born as the Holy Empire with Roman longing to lose its history in a Stalinist monstrosity of

69

materialism – how can that ever be accepted by the people in the states that survive, which are derived from an old culture?

Reunification should be an opportunity to re-establish the old Prussian civilising spirit which originally bestowed Roman Catholic Christianity on the East – that is, Poland:

> The reunification which defines the heart, which the heart signifies, needs a much greater embrace that will lead to mutual benefit. It also includes the reconciliation with the Polish people over centuries . . . It is not the borders of 1937, which led to the last war, that describe the German empire, but rather the human culture from before 1914 which should be the occasion for us to help precisely there, no matter who lives there today . . . Let us establish partnerships with Bohemia, the Polish inheritors of former German provinces, as preferred relatives instead of as children. For us it is not a question of the men, which is accidental, but of the land . . . Without the Poles, no Prussia; without Germany, no Christian Poland.

As Syberberg points out, the Prussian ethos has never been marked by the revanchism of Marxist ideologies, since in Prussia 'many families live well together as the neighbours of former enemies'.

Syberberg considers the model of Prussian Germany as an essential one for the cultural development of the nation, and German music in particular as a quintessential form of its art: 'always where this art came closest to [music] in Germany it was incomparably one with itself: music in things, in pictures, in words, in houses, in Nature'. The development of the classical art of the past was possible since it emulated with humility an ideal in an imperfect world: 'the classical epochs, independently of the misery of the individual martyrdom of their art's creators, understood their artistic ideal as the world's claim to spiritual happiness'. On the other hand, 'Art today is the model of the poverty of a democratic reality which is praised as the best of all worlds, masking its lies in such a form that it must preach the art of ugliness as truth'. Thus, the modern Germans would do well to bear in mind the image of Prussia as a 'counter-image' to the democratic present, as a 'phantom image of art, a purity of an entirely different character'.

Syberberg's final exhortations to his readers are thus to recognise the genuine sources of art in Nature and the homeland. Only thus can Germans revive the old traditions and the old artistic ideals of beauty, truth, and goodness. As a method of cultural regeneration, Syberberg recommends a return to *'Heimat* (homeland), *Reich, Nation, Provinzen* (provinces), *Deutschland'*, to a 'unifying community, an organic community of people, state, and nature'. The destiny of the Germans is a higher one than the democratic downfall to which they have been condemned by the Marxists and Americans, for the Germans are, in Syberberg's words, 'the men who sacrifice their life to the eternity of art', and were merely used by the world-spirit, which

> goes over corpses, and art burns up the world . . . In the end, the eagle shakes the dust off its wings and flies towards the Sun . . . renewing itself for new deeds.

It is true that the modern German has been re-educated and sated with material prosperity, and forced to give up everything that was once good and valid. However, Syberberg reminds us that

> they are also rich in quite another way, for the experiences of the humiliating defeat, from the richness of the suffering through fear of bombs, and from the laments for fallen sons and fathers, and from the distress of sacrificed daughters and wives and lost lands . . .

Their awareness of the loss of their own natural character must re-emerge in the newly reunified Germany to liberate the Germans from American colonisation; primarily the 'anti-fascist' indoctrination of Adorno's cultural Marxism, which began at the end of the last war:

> The Germans must – and it seems as if they are not allowed to – re-establish the lost empires from inside as well, if they

wish to make a virtue of their distress, and to establish this loss as a virtue of art. But the loss of precisely this virtue made them poor and needy. And the Marshall Plan of re-education enticed them to alien fields of art. It will depend on what they make of an aesthetics based on the excitements of the cheap and quick and comfortable, also in the depth of the space of the lost provinces of their heart, secretly certain of their unbroken mission.

We see from Syberberg's lament for Prussian Germany that, if Europe as a whole should be revived from its post-war moribund stupor, it must, at all costs, resist the present American control of the continent that began with the financial and military assistance it received through the Marshall Plan. It must return to the native ways of thought and feeling of the Europeans, that are based not on mechanical technology and trade but on the natural orders – aristocratic and religious – of society. Syberberg's analyses of art and society in Europe after the war reveal that the principal cultural dilemma of today is indeed one wherein the German and European question – based on the possibility of an artistic regeneration in a reunified Germany, and in the larger European community in general – is pitted against the withering Jewish-American international economic enterprise. The impossibility of developing true culture under a democratic system is obvious given the commercial, immoral, and eventually criminal foundations of this system. True art can develop only under a system that considers the land as the source of its culture, and whose rulers resemble the royal patrons of the past who, as Syberberg points out, were not men characterised by 'envy and hatred', as those in power today are. The liberation of Europe from its present Jewish-American rule is thus a precondition for its re-emergence as the leading civilised – and civilising – power in a world that is threatened today with the globalised stultification of mankind.

IV

The Supremacy of the West:
A Review of Two Studies by
Ricardo Duchesne and Niall Ferguson[1]

In 2011, two major scholarly works appeared that attempted to investigate the sources of Western supremacy in the modern world, especially in view of the recent rise of China as a potential threat to this supremacy. These are the Puerto Rican-Canadian social historian Ricardo Duchesne's *The Uniqueness of Western Civilization*[2] and the British economic historian Niall Ferguson's *Civilisation: The West and the Rest*.[3] Though focused on the same subject of Western dominance, Duchesne's thesis is a rather more ponderous socio-philosophical one extolling the so-called 'aristocratic egalitarianism' of the Euro-

---

[1] This essay was published as 'Reflections on the Supremacy of the West: A Critique of Ricardo Duchesne and Niall Ferguson' in *Counter-Currents*, April 26, 2019 (www.counter-currents.com/2019/04/ reflections-on-the-supremacy-of-the-west/).

[2] Ricardo Duchesne, *The Uniqueness of Western Civilization* (Leiden–Boston: Brill, 2011).

[3] Niall Ferguson, *Civilization: The West and the Rest* (New York: Penguin Books, 2011).

peans from the fourth millennium BC up to the modern age. Duchesne devotes much (perhaps too much) time to summarising and citing from numerous other scholarly works on the social history and political philosophy of Europe – and this makes it perhaps a useful reference book for students of European historical sociology. On the other hand, Ferguson's study is a more colourful and anecdotal one, since it was originally designed to be accompanied by a television series, the *BBC*'s six-part *Civilization*. The historical scope of Ferguson's defence of capitalism, including its colonial effects, is also more limited than Duchesne's – extending from the Renaissance and Protestant Reformation up to the present day.

According to Duchesne, the five main objectives of his work are, first, to trace the multicultural ideological sources that have impelled the 'provincialisation' of the history of Western civilisation; second, to discount the 'similarities' noted by anti-Eurocentric scholars between the developments of the Western and non-Western worlds; third, to demonstrate that 'the West has always existed in a state of variance from the rest of the world's cultures'; fourth, to relate the rise of the West to its liberal-democratic culture; and fifth, to trace the West's creativity back to the aristocratic egalitarianism of the ancient Indo-Europeans' society.

The first two chapters deal with the first objective listed above, as well as with the particular conflict between Eurocentric and Sinocentric historiography. Since I have little interest, or expertise, in Sinology and consider this entire section to be an unnecessary deference to multi-culturalist academics, I shall not comment on it in detail.

The second section of the book (Chapters 3, 4, and 5), dealing with the West's industrial and scientific progress and its developed rationalism, corresponds to the second, third, and fourth of the author's objectives. Since this is one of the major parts of the work, a closer look at it is in order. It is the author's intention here to demonstrate that the multi-faceted flowering of Western civilisation, and its 'modernity', are especially due to its 'ideal of freedom, and the ideal of a critical, self-reflexive public culture'.[4]

In tracing the advances of the West in science and industry, Duchesne points to Margaret Jacob's thesis[5] that

> Calvinism, more than any other religious current within Christianity, endowed scientific knowledge with millenarian importance. This religious-utilitarian ethos preached by the Quakers and liberal Anglicans cannot be ignored in our efforts to understand why the *first* successful application of modern science occurred in Britain.[6]

He stresses also the development of something like a free trade economy in Britain after the 'Glorious' Revolution of 1688:

> [T]he triumph of Parliament over the kings after the Glorious Revolution of 1688 . . . resulted in the incorporation of mercantile elites into the power-seeking aims and responsibilities of the state. This commercial-national-representative culture fostered a far more sophisticated financial system, such as stock exchanges and a national bank able to float massive loans.[7]

At the same time, the increase in economic power was accompanied by the rise of military might. Duchesne cites, for instance, Charles Tilly, who had argued in *Coercion, Capital, and European States, AD 990–1990*[8] that

> the global dynamic of European states was a result of the fusion of both capitalism and military might, of the military and political ambitions of the state, and of the economic interests

---

[4] Duchesne, *The Uniqueness of Western Civilization*, p. 225.

[5] Margaret Jacob, *Scientific Culture and the Making of the Industrial West* (New York: Oxford University Press, 1997).

[6] Duchesne, *The Uniqueness of Western Civilization*, p. 202.

[7] *Ibid.*, p. 225.

[8] Charles Tilly, *Coercion, Capital, and European States, AD 990-1990* (Cambridge, MA: Blackwell, 2002).

of the mercantile elites. Those nation states that were able to draw extensively on the wealth created by capitalists – by co-opting the bourgeoisie as a partner in the state – were the most successful ones in increasing their concentration of the means of coercion against their foes.[9]

Duchesne also associates the scientific and industrial revolutions of the West with the rise of rationalism in the West:

> A Western scientist is not simply or minimally motivated by a drive to master nature and increase productivity, but is also a person who believes that it is possible to augment one's knowledge of the natural world within a community of open inquiry and independent verification. If nature is something we can explore and understand, then we have elevated the rational abilities of humans; we are no longer on a par with the natural world, we are free to employ our capacities to see into nature's workings and make use of its powers.[10]

The focus on rationalism as a major driving force of modern capitalism was also present in Max Weber's well-known work, *Die protestantische Ethik und der Geist des Kapitalismus*, which had pointed to Protestantism as the source of the rational entrepreneurship of Western man. As Duchesne summarises it, 'Calvinism took this process further by abandoning the "otherworldly" asceticism of early Christianity (and Hinduism) and promoting instead a "this-worldly" religion that celebrated the rational mastery of the world as an ideal'. However, following other Jewish scholars like Reinhard Bendix[11] and John Love,[12] Duchesne himself attempts to identify the rationalistic core of

---

[9] Duchesne, *The Uniqueness of Western Civilization*, p. 215.

[10] *Ibid.*, p. 239.

[11] Reinhard Bendix, *Max Weber: An Intellectual Portrait* (Berkeley: University of California Press, 1977).

[12] John Love, 'Max Weber's Ancient Judaism', in *The Cambridge Companion to Weber*, ed. Stephen Turner (Cambridge: Cambridge University Press, 2000).

the West not in Christian learning, but in ancient Judaism. In fact, in his *General Economic History*, Weber too had suggested that 'Judaism was nonetheless of notable significance for modern rational capitalism, insofar as it transmitted to Christianity the latter's hostility to magic'.[13]

However, Duchesne reminds his readers also of Gary Abraham's essay, 'Max Weber on "Jewish Rationalism" and the Jewish Question' (1988),[14] which had maintained that Weber had not argued that there was a direct relationship between 'Old Testament rationalism' and the rise of modern capitalism (with its disciplined rationalisation of production). On the other hand, Weber had noted that the caste-like separation of the Jews from their surroundings made them a perpetual guest-people more interested in the preservation of their identity than in the encouragement of modernity. This 'pariah status' promoted, on the one hand, a strong adherence to the ethical prescriptions of Judaism, in a rationalistic and a legalistic manner, but, on the other, it 'led to the Jewish people's retaining a different economic morality for its relations with strangers than with fellow Jews' (as Weber wrote in the long section on 'The Sociology of Jews and Judaism' in *Economy and Society*).[15]

Duchesne further points out that Jonathan Israel had, in his *Radical Enlightenment: Philosophy and the Making of Modernity, 1650–1750*,[16] sought to demonstrate that the 'decisive breakthrough of modern rationalism and secularization' occurred in the period 1680–1750, for it was then that 'the primacy of confessional theology and scholastic Aristotelianism . . . finally disintegrated' and that the radical ideas revolving around Spinoza and Spinozism became a European-wide

---

[13] Duchesne, *The Uniqueness of Western Civilization*, p. 259.

[14] Gary Abraham, 'Max Weber on "Jewish Rationalism" and the Jewish Question', *International Journal of Politics, Culture, and Society*, Vol. 1, No. 3 (Spring, 1988), pp. 358-391.

[15] Duchesne, *The Uniqueness of Western Civilization*, p. 258.

[16] Jonathan I. Israel, *Radical Enlightenment: Philosophy and the Making of Modernity, 1650–1750* (Oxford: Oxford University Press, 2001).

movement that 'demolished all legitimation of monarchy, aristocracy, woman's subordination to man, ecclesiastical authority, and slavery'.[17]

This growing rationalism, which seems to have been impelled in no small part by the Jews in European society, found its ultimate expression in liberal-democratic political institutions. As Duchesne puts it: 'the rise of the West is the story of the realization of humans who think of themselves as self-determining and therefore accept as authoritative only those norms and institutions that can be seen to be congenial with their awareness of themselves as free and rational agents'.[18] In addition, Duchesne points to Charles Taylor's argument[19] that 'the affirmation of ordinary life' was one of the essential legacies of the Protestant movement: 'This affirmation of everyday life, along with the relative devaluing of the classical and medieval aristocratic ethic of military honour and intellectual contemplation, involved a new sensitivity to work and family life'.[20] Although this is not the purpose of Duchesne's sprawling study, we may discern from the author's scrupulous collation of scholarly views how Judaism and Protestantism were instrumental in the transformation of the original aristocratic ethos of the Indo-Europeans into the modern liberal one.

The last section of Duchesne's book (chapters 6, 7, and 8) deals with Hegelian and post-Hegelian interpretations of the rise of the West through its 'Faustian' desire for knowledge and the 'restlessness' of its spirit to subdue the outer world to its ends. The idea of indefinite progress was lacking in the Eastern civilisations, and thus hindered them from advancing as rapidly as the West did. In other words, the forces of tradition – that which is sought after today by the so-called 'Traditionalists' – are indeed what prevented the Eastern nations and empires

---

[17] Duchesne, *The Uniqueness of Western Civilization*, p. 282.

[18] *Ibid.*, p. 270.

[19] Charles Taylor, *Sources of the Self: The Making of the Modern Identity* (Cambridge: Cambridge University Press, 1989).

[20] Duchesne, *The Uniqueness of Western Civilization*, p. 278.

from prevailing as world-powers. Charles Murray, who had, in his *Human Accomplishment: The Pursuit of Excellence in the Arts and Sciences, 800 BC to 1950*,[21] undertaken the rather confounding task of tabulating all of man's most significant works through the ages, believed that it was Christian thought in particular that propelled the West's individualism. According to Murray, however, one of the disastrous consequences of the Protestant Reformation was that it led to a progressive secularisation of Western society so that, after 1950, increasing atheism was accompanied by a concomitant lack of creativity. Murray's cataloguing enterprise may seem a rather foolish one, but his stress on religion is nevertheless precious.

Rather than elaborating on this emphasis, however, Duchesne favours instead G. W. F. Hegel's dynamic view, in his *Phänomenologie des Geistes* (Phenomenology of the Spirit, 1807), of the march of a self-realising 'Reason' through 'Time'. Hegel's fantastic view of what Indians would call 'Kali Yuga' civilisations as evidence of a progressive evolution of human reason is clearly an embarrassing philosophical fiction, but Duchesne does not distinguish human creativity from technological invention any more clearly than Hegel did. He ventures to declare instead that his concern with the rise of 'individualism' is indeed with the rise of the philosophical sense of the Self itself among the Europeans. This will certainly be bewildering to anybody who has studied the thorough-going and profound discussions of the Self in the sacred literature of the Indians, such as the Upanishads, that date back thousands of years. The relatively late rise of awareness of the Self among the Europeans compared to the Indians is hard to explain if they were both originally members of the same family of ancient Indo-Europeans in the Pontic steppe.

Duchesne follows Hegel in believing that the uniqueness of the Western mind derives from the relative freedom and autonomy from centralised authority of the democratic city-states

---

[21] Charles Murray, *Human Accomplishment: The Pursuit of Excellence in the Arts and Sciences, 800 BC to 1950* (New York: HarperCollins, 2003).

of ancient Greece. This rise of individualism was made possible, in the Hegelian view, by the rise of the sense of freedom, which was guaranteed only by the modern liberal-democratic state. However, Hegel also believed that history was made by great historical personalities like Alexander and Napoleon – which rather suggests that he was outlining a history of mastery and slavery and not of liberal democracy. Duchesne attempts to solve this conundrum by positing an imagined aristocratic society of the ancient Indo-Europeans that fostered equality among superior members of that society. According to him, it was the spirited combat between equally strong men who were contemptuous of death and desirous only to gain the 'recognition' of peers and glory that gradually gave rise to self-consciousness itself.

Duchesne's individualistic Western man is thus said to arise not from Christianity, as Murray had suggested, but from what Duchesne calls the aristocratic 'egalitarianism', and freedom, of the most ancient Indo-European societies that existed in the Pontic steppe. However, the fragmentary archaeological and literary evidence that we possess from the fourth millennium BC can hardly be adduced to construct elaborate sociological theories of the cultures then extant, and this section of Duchesne's work must, in the final analysis, be counted as an exercice in sociological fantasy.

Following William McNeill,[22] Duchesne imagines that the bearers of Western civilisation were the nomadic pastoral peoples of the Pontic steppe. He also adduces David Anthony's work,[23] which had speculated that the movements of the nomadic Indo-Europeans in the Pontic steppe southwards may explain an original contact between the steppe cultures and the civilisations of the Near East in the middle of the fourth

---

[22] William McNeill, *The Rise of the West: A History of the Human Community* (Chicago: University of Chicago Press, 1963).

[23] David W. Anthony, *The Horse, the Wheel, and Language: How Bronze-Age Riders from the Eurasian Steppes Shaped the Modern World* (Princeton: Princeton University Press, 2007).

millennium BC. But while it is possible that the advanced Uruk cultures of Sumer and of Early Dynastic Egypt, which are Hamitic, might have had some Indo-European element in them (such as, notably, that group which some scholars have called the 'Dynastic Race'),[24] it is still puzzling why the bearers of the more finely-articulated high cultures of Mesopotamia and Egypt always spoke agglutinative Hamitic and Hurrian languages rather than the inflected ones of imposingly warlike Russian elements within their societies.

Indeed, we are rather ignorant of the cultural development of the Indo-Europeans when they were in the Pontic steppe. Their religious traditions are not attested until the Āryan peoples come into contact with the developed urban civilisations of the south – in India, Mesopotamia, and the Mediterranean. We may, in this context, also recall Megasthenes' account of the early Indians:

> The Indians were in old times nomadic, like those Scythians who did not till the soil, but roamed about in their wagons, as the seasons varied, from one part of Scythia to another, neither dwelling in towns nor worshipping in temples; and that the Indians likewise had neither towns nor temples of the gods, but were so barbarous that they wore the skins of such wild animals as they could kill . . . they subsisted also on such wild animals as they could catch, eating the flesh raw, – before, at least, the coming of Dionysus into India. Dionysus, however, when he came and had conquered the people, founded cities and gave laws to these cities, and introduced the use of wine among the Indians, as he had done among the Greeks, and taught them to sow the land, himself supplying seeds for the purpose.[25]

---

[24] See, for instance, Alexander Jacob, 'The "Dynastic Race" and the Biblical Japheth', Parts I and II, *Ancient Origins*, 13-14 Oct. 2017 (www.ancient-origins.net./human-origins-religions/dynastic-race-and-biblical-japheth-part-i-after-deluge-008956).

[25] See Arrian, *Indica*, VII, in R. C. Majumdar, *The Classical Accounts of India* (Calcutta: Firma K. L. Mukhopadhyay, 1960), p. 220f.

Since Dionysus is the same as the solar god of the Mesopotamians, An, and the Egyptian Horus the Elder-Osiris,[26] and the earliest evidence of the Dravidian god, Muruga, in India reveals a Dionysiac deity, we may assume that the cultural contact being referred to by Megasthenes is that between the early Indo-Scythian settlers of India and Elamite Dravidians/Hurrians from the Zagros region.[27]

Duchesne, however, points to J. P. Mallory and Marija Gimbutas, who had represented the Indo-Europeans as invading warriors in the ancient Middle East and Mediterranean. Mallory had suggested that, in the case of the colonisation of Europe, the adoption of Indo-European speech by the Old Europeans was due to 'the greater vitality and potential for growth of the pastoral economy'. According to him, the native population became bilingual, 'speaking the Indo-European language in the market place or at ceremonial centers in order to obtain better access to goods, status, ritual, and security'.[28]

The nomadic character of the Pontic Indo-Europeans is indeed confirmed by their typical horse-riding affiliations, the horse having first been domesticated in the fifth millennium BC in the Pontic steppe. The veneration of the horse among the Indo-Iranians, or Āryans, is attested by the important Ashwamedha sacrifice among the Indo-Āryans and the numerous names ending in -aspa (horse) among the Iranians. However, Anthony had pointed to the fact that the Corded Ware culture that prevailed in northern Europe in the third millennium BC gave evidence of battle-axes that are not attested in the Yamnaya culture (from 3400 BC) of the Pontic steppe. So there is no concrete evidence of the 'warlike' nature of the original Indo-European society north of the Black Sea, as Duchesne would like us to imagine. Further, though Anthony thinks that the chariot may have appeared in the Pontic steppe already in

---

[26] See Alexander Jacob, *Ātman: A Reconstruction of the Solar Cosmology of the Indo-Europeans* (Hildesheim: Georg Olms, 2005), Chapter XII.

[27] *Ibid.*, Introduction.

[28] Duchesne, *The Uniqueness of Western Civilization*, p. 360.

the third millennium BC, the typical Āryan association with chariots is not fully confirmed until the second millennium and the spread of the Indo-Iranians (with names revealing their charioteering affiliations) and the coming of the Mycenean Greeks around 1600 BC.

Duchesne then considers Colin Renfrew's view that the first civilisations of India and Europe's regions were also Indo-Europeans from Anatolia, who excelled in farming rather than war, and that the Indo-European who later invaded these parts were a group that had moved north and east of the Black Sea, probably very early, since they maintained a nomadic pastoral rather than agrarian culture there. The group of Indo-Europeans that arrived later may have borne more archaic horse-riding traits and contributed to the development of Anatolian and European cultures, though they may have gradually adopted the agricultural habits and benefits of the earlier groups here. Their sojourn in Anatolia would have turned them into a farming society, and their westward movements into Europe were probably propelled by cultivating and civilising impulses rather than warlike ones, as Duchesne tends to think.

This possibility seems to accord with evidence from the Prologue to Snorri Sturluson's thirteenth-century *Prose Edda,* where we are told that the languages of central and northern Europe were brought there by Aesir led by Wotan, who migrated from north of the Black Sea to Anatolia, and then to the Balkans and northern Europe. This migration may be dated to around the Trojan War (ca. twelfth century BC), since Snorri mentions King Priam in his account.

Duchesne, however, wishes to maintain a stark distinction between the autocratic monarchies of the ancient Near East and the incoming Indo-Europeans, who, according to him, were aristocratic insofar as they valued not the despotic rule of a monarch, but personal heroism and 'a strong ethos of aristocratic egalitarianism against despotic rule'. He concedes that the original Indo-European aristocratic ethos may have been gradually transformed in India and Iran so that it finally became autocratic kingship and imperialism.[29] Duchesne's focus on the warrior bases of European society prevents him from investigating the reasons why the brāhmans rather than the kshatriyas were the preeminent element in ancient Indian society.

Interestingly, however – in the course of this discussion of the warlike nature of the ancient Europeans – Duchesne pauses to consider the phenomenon of tragedy among the Greeks. He believes that, since tragedy emerges as a literary form only among the Greeks, such a heroic ethos prevailed only among the Western Indo-Europeans:

> Heroism and tragedy require a culture in which some individuals are free to set themselves apart from others. Tragedy is a form of literature that expresses acutely the inescapable sacrifices and limitations entailed in the human effort to achieve greatness. This sense of limitation grows not out of a feeling of enslavement to mysterious forces but out of a realization that individuals who covet immortal fame are fated to engage in hubristic acts which inevitably bring about suffering, disappointment, and early death.[30]

Similarly, in the case of epic poetry, 'the political structure of the ancient Near East was autocratic, and . . . there was no room in the states of Mesopotamia for the cultivation of true heroic epics.'[31]

Duchesne ignores the Dionysiac religious sources of the rise of Greek tragedy and does not seem to be at all aware that the tragic sense does not arise from combating gladiators, but from men of superior psychological constitution who possess an innate disdain for worldly life not unrelated to the *contemptus mundi* of the mediaeval Christian thinkers. The true creators of art, as well as of science, philosophy, and politics – in ancient Indo-European society as well as in more modern – are those who

---

[29] *Ibid.*, p. 377ff.

[30] *Ibid.*, p. 404.

[31] *Ibid.*, p. 402.

are imbued with a sense of the imperfection of human life, but also of the need to nevertheless elevate this life towards the perfection of the divine. The ancient caste-distinctions between the priests/warriors and the rest of the people were indeed derived from the presence or absence of this sense. The brāhmans are characterised by the quality of *sattva* (associated with 'perfect being' and 'spirit') because they are closer to the divine reality, while the people in general are marked by *tamas*, denoting the sluggishness of matter.

Proceeding with his paean to Indo-European individualism, Duchesne maintains that a society ruled by martial, honour-loving aristocrats leads to a spirit of competition among artists as well. However, this thesis bears as little resemblance to the reality of Greek art as Duchesne's thesis concerning Greek tragedy does. The sacred nature of works of art in antiquity, prominently portrayed in the numerous depictions of gods, is completely ignored by the author.

Duchesne declares that the typical form of government of the ancient Europeans should not be identified, as has hitherto been done by Classicists, with the Greek democracy of the sixth century BC but rather with the earlier aristocratic Mycenaean world reflected in Homer's *Iliad*. According to him, the Homeric spirit is that of 'the Indo-European chieftains who took over the Greek mainland in the second millennium, and founded Mycenaean culture', and that the latter carried with them the warlike aristocratic ethos of the ancient Indo-Europeans of the fourth and third millennia when they were still located in the Pontic steppe. Though the Indo-Europeans were originally a nomadic people, their contact with farming communities in the Mediterranean caused them to rule the local population, impose their language on them, and establish kingdoms or chiefdoms there.

Despite this effort to conjure up a more heroic Indo-European past, Duchesne spends much time discussing the democratic excellence of the Greek city-states:

the constitution of the Greeks states was democratic. Now, it is true that, in spite of the constitutional incorporation of all male citizens into the government, most Greek poleis remained oligarchic in actuality. Constitutionally, participation in the public assemblies was denied to slaves, resident aliens, and women; and, of the male citizens (roughly one-third of the population) who enjoyed rights of self-government, it was really a small elite of aristocratic families who had the means and connections to regulate the affairs of the state. Nevertheless, particularly in the case of 5th century Athens, the extent to which citizens participated in every decision of the state was remarkable.[32]

He then proceeds to demonstrate that 'sovereignty in Republican Rome was invested in the aristocratic Senate and in the Tribunes of the people'.[33] In other words, he envisages the *politeia* of Greece and Rome to have been an aristocratic democracy that shunned monarchy.

Duchesne seems to ignore the conditional historical dependence of every aristocracy on a monarchy. Even the Roman Republic was preceded by sacred monarchs – *pontifices* – whose advisory council, the Senate, indeed furnished the later Republic with its aristocratic senators. There is no evidence in the Indo-Iranian sacred literature, either, of any predominance of the Indic kshatriya or Avestan rathaeshtār in the earliest Āryan societies. The term 'kshatriya' is derived from *kshatra*, which means sovereignty, and that is normally wielded by a king; 'rathaeshtār' merely signifies a driver of a *ratha*, or chariot. The warrior caste among the Āryans is thus intimately allied to the kingly. And kingship among the Āryans was divine, as is evident in the Rājasūya sacrifice among the Indo-Āryans, where the king assumes the role of the Sun in the course of the consecration rituals.[34] In this apotheosis, he is indissociably amalgamated with the first caste, which is that of the brāhman or āthravan, who represents Agni, the fiery force within the Sun.

Duchesne expands on his romantic hypothesis about the

---

[32] *Ibid.*

[33] *Ibid.*

[34] See Alexander Jacob, *Brahman: A Study of the Solar Rituals of the Indo-Europeans* (Hildesheim: Georg Olms, 2012), Chapter IX.

migrations southwards from the Pontic steppe by suggesting that they were impelled not merely by economic constraints, but also by the restless, warlike nature of these people, which made them seek glory and honour in battle and to fight in the frenzied 'berserker' style of the Germans. He does not consider, however, why the Greeks and Romans, who were also – according to him – of the same stock, would consider the Germans 'barbarians' for doing so. Relying partly on the martial objects buried in the graves of the early Indo-Europeans, he proclaims that '[t]he Indo-European cultures which spread throughout Europe (2800–1300 BC) were all "Bronze Age" chiefdoms ... chief-level societies of increasing complexity ruled by aristocratic elites'.[35] Likewise 'both the Corded Ware and the Bell Beaker cultures of early Bronze Age Europe (from about 3000 BC) were dominated by an upper stratum of aristocrats in which objects of social prestige were used as grave goods'.[36]

But Duchesne is not content with emphasising this warrior-aristocratic nature of the ancient Indo-Europeans. He goes on to suggest that their well-developed spirit of individualism is equally a result of this nature. Indeed, he imagines that the very concept of the 'Self' is due to this individualistic excellence derived from warriors. But this is to discount the evidence of all of Indian philosophy, which has little relation to kshatriya adventures, but which was rather developed through ascetic Yogic meditational techniques. And an unphilosophical individualism, however aristocratic in origin, is naturally susceptible to degeneration into mere selfishness, if not rapacity.

Duchesne points out that Charles Taylor[37] had read Plato's philosophy as 'an effort to subordinate the warrior-citizen morality of strength, courage, and glory – which grew out of the berserker barbarian past – to a philosophical morality of dispassionate deliberation'.[38] But Duchesne himself maintains that the

---

[35] *Ibid.*, p. 390.

[36] *Ibid.*, p. 446.

[37] *Op. cit.*

[38] *Ibid.*, p. 443.

Homeric heroes, as well as the Germanic berserkers, were already self-conscious to a high degree. The entire derivation of a presumed Indo-European psychological character from a single Greek epic, or from fragmentary Nordic sagas which deal with diverse mythological and political events, is rather implausible. Furthermore, Duchesne conflates individualism with 'the restlessness of barbarian individuals', and considers the latter as

> the primordial source of all that has been noble and great in Western civilization. Plato was the product of this individualism; his effort to subordinate the warrior ethos to the faculty of reason was an expression of his desire to achieve rational mastery.[39]

In other words, Plato himself becomes the winner in a competition with warriors for social pre-eminence, in Duchesne's view.

Relying further on Alexandre Kojève and Francis Fukuyama, Duchesne identifies the spirited, or thymotic, part of the tripartite soul as that which causes higher men to seek the recognition of equally elevated peers. 'What aristocrats desire is recognition of their worth and dignity by other masters possessing equal worth and dignity.'[40] He then adduces Nietzsche's theory that '[t]he Homeric and classical inhabitants of city-states brought these primordial drives under "measure" and self-control, re-channeling their will to power into creative-cultural venues'.[41] Thus all culture may be said to derive from the warrior caste of the ancient Indo-Europeans.

At this point, however, Duchesne refers to Kojève's interesting thesis[42] that, 'while the masters cannot go beyond their own heroic world-view their inferiors or slaves gradually begin

---

[39] *Ibid.*, p. 441.

[40] *Ibid.*, p. 423.

[41] *Ibid.*, p. 444.

[42] Alexandre Kojève, ed. Allan Bloom, tr. James Nichols, Jr., *Introduction to the Reading of Hegel: Lectures on the Phenomenology of Spirit* (New York: Basic Books, 1969), compiled from lectures given by the autor between 1933 and 1939.

to acquire a sort of freedom by mastering their nature through their work that results in various forms of scientific invention and technology'. The slave, when he gradually turns into a bourgeois, 'engenders "abstract thought, science, technique, the arts – all these have their origin in the forced work of the slave."'[43] This vicarious self-mastery is, as we shall see in our reading of Ferguson, what characterised the earliest British 'servant' settlements in America, and points to the democratic – rather than aristocratic – nature of the 'supremacy' of the technologically advanced West.

However, continuing his 'aristocratic' social history of the West, Duchesne believes that Christian civilisation is also the result of a successful infusion of 'aristocratic' Germanic barbarian qualities into the Late Roman Empire:

> But the goal of the Church was to spiritualize the baser instincts of this class, not to extirpate and emasculate them. The highly-strung and obstinate aristocrat has been a fundamental source of destruction in Western history as well as the source of all that is good and inspiring.[44]

Nevertheless, when Duchesne concludes his panoramic study of aristocratic Indo-Europeans, he is forced to admit rather shamefacedly that modern liberalism must be seen

> as an effort to alter the aristocratic nature of Western man. In the West, the spirited or thymotic part of the soul was long free to play a dominant role both in its pristine existence through Indo-European barbarians and in its sublimated form through Greek, Roman, and Christian medieval times. This spirit was the force, the passion behind the restless and relentless style of rational discoursing, artistic creation, and expansionism of Europeans. But insomuch as this drive was contained and pacified – conceived as the rational pursuit of one's

---

[43] Duchesne, *The Uniqueness of Western Civilization*, p. 427.

[44] *Ibid.*, p. 481.

self-interest – the spirited part of the soul, I would ar-
gue, was demoted to being just one type of desire similar
to the appetitive desire for survival and comfort.[45]

The restlessness or thymotic excellence of Western man was
channeled into his lower biological needs:

> Accordingly, to the degree that the spirited part of the Wes-
> tern soul was suppressed by the ethical demands of modern
> democratic liberalism, re-channeled into economic inventive-
> ness, or confounded with bodily appetites, it became increa-
> singly difficult for scholars to attribute the restlessness of the
> West to this part of the soul. Since the restlessness of the West
> could not be attributed to biological drives equally present in
> all human beings, the tendency was to attribute it to the pure-
> ly rational part of the soul.[46]

He points to Weber's sociology in particular as an example of
the erroneous substitution of reason in place of restlessness as
the driving force of Western development:

> Max Weber is the best known classical exponent of the thesis
> that the development of the West was due to its "specific and
> peculiar" rationalism. As commendable as this interpretation
> is, I hope to have persuaded some that the roots of the West
> are to be found in a profoundly different aristocratic character
> that first came into the light of history in the Pontic steppes.[47]

It is not clear why Duchesne focuses on Weber, who was not
a philosopher, and why he fails to indict Baruch Spinoza – as
Israel had done[48] – for the elevation of the intellect to a supreme
role in the governance of the universe, or Sigmund Freud for the
liberation of the biological drives into a social ethos conducive

---

[45] *Ibid.*, p. 487.

[46] *Ibid.*

[47] *Ibid.*

[48] See above, p. 77.

to anarchy. Rather than ascribe the subversion of the Indo-European aristocratic society to Puritans like John Locke, or Rationalists like Spinoza, or psychoanalysts like Freud, Duchesne suggests that the characteristic restlessness of the Indo-Europeans – or their thymotic aspect – itself may have led to this degeneration. Western culture, according to him, 'has always been charged with tension, always striving to transcend itself, and thus always engaged in a fight against itself – a fight that would culminate in the nihilism, cultural relativism, weariness, and lack of faith in Western civilization that dominates today'.[49]

The problem with Duchesne's glorification of the thymotic or warrior-like aspect of Indo-European society is that he fails to understand that the warrior caste only derives its virtue from its association with the priestly or religious caste. Divorced from the latter, it is only too easily susceptible to degeneration through association with the lower unaristocratic, or popular, sections of society. The distinction that Duchesne forces in his study between aristocrats and monarchs is also a false one, since the two are indissociably connected to each other, and the priesthood represents the spiritual core of any true aristocracy. The people, insofar as they are ruled by *tamas*, represent Kojève's 'slaves', and the technological world that they create is informed by a Spinozistic understanding of Nature as God (*Deus sive Natura*). The celebration of the biological drives that Duchesne bemoans in modern liberal society, and that had been anticipated by Freud's psychology, is equally related to the Nature-oriented, *tāmasic* part of the soul.

∗∗∗

Another major defect of Duchesne's work is its failure to distinguish the European from the American West. His study is mostly centred on European history and philosophy and does not note the crucial differences between these and the society and culture developed in the New World. Niall Ferguson, on the

---

[49] *Ibid.*, p. 284.

other hand, elaborates more on the capitalism consummated in America, though he does not omit the origins of industrialism in Britain, or the various effects of European colonialism and totalitarianism. The transformation of what Duchesne called an aristocratic egalitarianism into liberal democracy is more precisely charted in Ferguson's survey of the history of Western capitalism.

According to Ferguson, the main achievements of the West that elevated it above 'the rest' and allowed it to dominate the latter were competition, science, property rights, medicine, the consumer society, and the work ethic – all of which he comically terms the West's six 'killer apps'. We notice that, in Ferguson's history, the competition that Duchesne noticed as an adjunct of the individualism of early aristocratic societies is focused on the fact of decentralisation 'of both political and economic life, which created the launch-pad for both nation-states and capitalism'. According to Ferguson, China in the fifteenth century under the Ming Dynasty could already boast of many technological innovations, and was even capable of exploring the seas and conducting international trade. Yet it failed to do so because of the centralised bureaucracy of that dynasty, or because, as Max Weber had put it in *Konfuzianismus und Taoismus* (Confucianism and Taoism, 1915), Confucian rationalism meant 'rational adjustment to the world', as opposed to the Western concept of 'rational mastery of the world'. The European adventurers, unlike their Chinese counterparts, were given a free hand in a time of warring European states that precluded a centralised power on the continent. Further, the nascent banking institutions in England and Holland began to wield a power that was almost independent of royal rule. This enabled the establishment of the Dutch East India Company and the British East India Company as capitalist corporations. The spirit of competition between the various sea-faring European nations allowed European trade and colonisation in the East to proceed apace.

The section on science compares the temporary achievements of Ottoman Turkey with the more enduring successes of the

West, while that on medicine recounts the extension of medical science within the African colonies, including the German experiments in what Ferguson considers to be racialist pseudo-science. Ferguson particularly mentions Dr. Eugen Fischer (the teacher of the notorious Josef Mengele) as a proponent of this branch of medicine, which justified the cruel treatment of Africans, just as it later did that of European minorities during the Third Reich.

The section on property rights is closely associated with Ferguson's insistence on the rule of law and representational government as indispensable constituents of civilisation. In this section, he focuses mainly on the early American settlements, which attracted Britain's lower classes – as well as the persecuted minorities of other European countries – to the North American continent, with the promise of land that could be acquired without any of the warlike qualifications that were required to attain the aristocratic estates of the early Europeans. American democracy was based on the rule of law to the extent that it endorsed 'the sanctity of individual freedom and the security of private property rights, ensured by representative, constitutional government'.[50] It was thus essentially a property-owners' democracy. As Locke had phrased it, 'The great and chief end therefore, of Men's uniting into Commonwealths . . . is the preservation of their Property'. Freedom, in Locke's view, was a man's 'Liberty to dispose, and order, as he lists, his Person, Actions, Possessions, and his whole Property, within the Allowance of those Laws under which he is; and therein not to be subject to the arbitrary Will of another'.[51]

This approach to democracy in North America differed essentially from the socio-political system prevailing in Iberian South America. Whereas the land that was cultivated by the European settlers of North America was fully appropriated from the indigenous peoples of the continent, in South America the indigenous peoples were made to work the land that was owned by a small European elite:

---

[50] Ferguson, *Civilization*, p. 97.

[51] *Ibid.*, p. 96.

Unlike in British colonies like Carolina, where acres were widely distributed, in Spanish America it was the right to exploit the indigenous people that was granted to a tiny elite.[52]

Thus, '[i]n South America the Indians worked the land. In North America they lost it'.[53]

Ferguson also considers the Roman Catholicism associated with the Spanish and Portuguese imperialism as defective, since it represented

> fundamentally a monopoly of another sort. North America, on the other hand, became home to numerous Protestant sects; dissent and diversity were among the organizing principles of British settlement. This had its shadow side (the Salem witchcraft trials spring to mind), but the clear benefit was the creation of a society of merchants and farmers committed to religious as well as political freedom.[54]

Ferguson's libertarianism makes him believe that the Americans – who have in fact established a quasi-commercial network of countless Protestant churches – are still religious, whereas modern-day Europeans have lost their religious associations more easily. But the religiosity of the Protestant sects is clearly in doubt, and the increasing lack of religiosity of the Europeans who are still rooted in their rich historical traditions is indeed much less a cause for alarm than what Ferguson himself calls 'a kind of consumer Christianity that verges on Wal-Mart worship'.[55]

Further, in spite of the incompatibility of the centralised rule of the Spanish crown and the Catholic Church with liberal democracy as Ferguson understands it, he points to the fact that Brazil, in spite of its multi-racialist population, has recently

---

[52] *Ibid.*, p. 113.

[53] *Ibid.*, p. 119.

[54] *Ibid.*, p. 114.

[55] *Ibid.*, p. 276.

managed to achieve an impressive economic level:

> Meanwhile, one of the most dynamic economies in the world is that of multi-coloured Brazil. The key to success in Brazil – still among the world's most unequal societies – has been long-overdue reform to give a rising share of the population a chance to own property and make money. After more than a century of over-reliance on protectionism, import substitution and other forms of state intervention, most of Latin America – with the sorry exception of Venezuela – has achieved higher growth since the 1980s with a combination of privatization, foreign investment and export orientation.[56]

Ferguson does not wonder why all these changes in the direction of American-style capitalism have not resulted in a decrease in poverty among the vast majority of the South American population. And he does not realise, either, that the society established by the Iberians in the south was more truly aristocratic than the blatantly democratic one founded by the British in the north, since the South American colonies were ruled originally by the two truly aristocratic segments of society, the Crown and the Church, and never devoted itself to the technological advancement typical of the 'slaves' discussed by Kojève and Duchesne.

The section on consumerism focuses on the relation between the consumer society and the Industrial Revolution, which increased Europeans' incomes through the increase in 'the productivity of land, labour and capital'. While the establishment of large industries meant a widening gap between the bourgeois capitalist industrialists and the labourers, the latter too gradually increased their wages and ability to consume the material benefits of mechanised industry. However, the concomitant reduction of social relations to what Thomas Carlyle called a 'cash nexus' inevitably led to the socialist revolutions of the nineteenth and twentieth centuries. Unfortunately, the dogmas of Communism as formulated by Marx and Engels included proscriptions of private property and private business ownership

---

[56] *Ibid.*, p. 139.

– dogmas that were in direct opposition to the third 'killer app' of property rights that characterised the American New World.

Ferguson then points with admiration to the fact that the innovative spirit of capitalism was not diminished in America even by the Great Depression:

> Innovation, the mainspring of industrial advance, did not slacken in the 1930s. New automobiles, radios and other consumer durables were proliferating . . . No less creative was the live, recorded and broadcast music business, once white Americans had discovered that black Americans had nearly all the best tunes.[57]

In the aftermath of the Depression, Germany and Russia sought to reduce unemployment through industrial expansion and rearmament. However, their concentration on heavy industry, infrastructure, and arms did not foster higher living standards or consumer spending. This is the reason, according to Ferguson, why Russia eventually lost the Cold War: 'centralized economic planning, though indispensable to success in the nuclear arms race, was wholly unsuited to the satisfaction of consumer wants.'[58] Ferguson gives as examples of America's victory the triumph of jeans and of rock music – the apparel and noise of the American proletariat – over the entire socio-political system of the Communists.

But all these tawdry American productions are precisely what a truly cultured person of the Old World – the real West – finds so repulsive in American society. The examples that Ferguson gives of the excellence of capitalism are blatant revelations of the general vulgarity, and lack of style, of the Americans, which can only be attributed to the plebeian character of American society from its very foundation. The spread of American proletarianism was crystallised in the revolutions of the sixties, when traditional Christian moral standards were overthrown in a Freudian orgy of free love and of real (as opposed to Duchesne's 'aristocratic') egalitarianism.

---

[57] *Ibid.*, pp. 229-230.

[58] *Ibid.*, p. 237.

The work ethic is defined by Ferguson as 'a moral framework and mode of activity derivable from (among other sources) Protestant Christianity'.[59] He points to the fact that Protestant countries in Europe fared better commercially than Catholic ones:

> There was indeed . . . a clear tendency after the Reformation for Protestant countries in Europe to grow faster than Catholic ones, so that by 1700 the former had clearly overtaken the latter in terms of per-capita income, and by 1940 people in Catholic countries were on average 40 per cent worse off than people in Protestant countries.[60]

Ferguson sees the explanation for this phenomenon in the fact that because of 'the central importance in Luther's thought of individual reading of the Bible, Protestantism encouraged literacy, not to mention printing, and these two things unquestionably encouraged economic development (the accumulation of 'human capital') as well as scientific study'.[61] But this is to discount the entire glorious edifice of learning propagated not only in Europe, but also in Europe's colonies by the Roman Catholic Church and the Jesuits.

Gradually, the industriousness of the Puritan settlers and their impulse to save were forgotten, and the work-ethic has now been replaced by the average American's reckless spending on credit. Ferguson does not investigate how the industry-based capitalism that may have been impelled by the Puritan work-ethic could have been transformed today into a financial 'gangster capitalism'. The worst he can observe in contemporary capitalism is that it is synonymous with rampant consumerism.

Furthermore, now that the 'killer apps' of international capitalist success have been distributed over much of the world, Ferguson wonders if Western civilisation can continue to maintain its supremacy, especially in light of China's rise in recent years.

---

[59] *Ibid.*, p. 13.

[60] *Ibid.*, p. 263.

[61] *Ibid.*

However, he concludes, much like Duchesne, by stressing the importance of having 'faith' in Western civilisation itself. The example of the past five hundred years is, according to Ferguson, itself a sufficient inspiration to its continuation:

> At its core, a civilization is the texts that are taught in its schools, learned by its students and recollected in times of tribulation. The civilization of China was once built on the teachings of Confucius. The civilization of Islam – of the cult of submission – is still built on the Koran. But what are the foundational texts of Western civilization that can bolster our belief in the almost boundless power of the free individual human being? . . . Maybe the real threat is posed not by the rise of China, Islam or CO_2 emissions, but by our own loss of faith in the civilization we inherited from our ancestors.[62]

However, the notion that a civilisation's continuance rests on the confidence that its participants have in it is a curious one that seems to be derived from the commercial phenomenon of 'investor confidence'. The grim possibility raised a little earlier in this work by Ferguson – but quickly rejected by him – is indeed more accurate: 'that all the achievements of Western civilisation – capitalism, science, the rule of law and democracy – have been reduced to nothing more profound than a spot of shopping'.

As in Duchesne's doubts about the end of the aristocratic spirit in 'nihilism, cultural relativism, weariness,' we are left once again with the disturbing feeling that the civilisation of the West today is powerful more by virtue of its 'slave' resourcefulness and restlessness than through any awareness of the religious foundations of Indo-European aristocracy or supremacy.

---

[62] *Ibid.*, pp. 324-325.

V

Aristocracy, Fascism
and the End of American History[1]

I

Francis Fukuyama, the Japanese-American intellectual spokes-
man for the Jewish-American 'Neoconservative' movement,
proclaimed in his book *The End of History and the Last Man*
that liberal democracy was the final socio-political form, since
earlier alternatives such as Fascism and Communism had prov-
en to be ideological failures, and liberty and equality had now
been established as universal norms. Fukuyama's view of history
moving in progressive political phases was of course first popu-
larised in the nineteenth century by German thinkers like G. W.
F. Hegel, Karl Marx, and their followers, who sought to discern
historiographical patterns in the vagaries of military and economic fortune, and to either celebrate or revolt against the current political status of their own nation – in their case, Germany.
To be sure, Hegel was somewhat more elevated than Marx in

---

[1] An earlier version of this essay was presented at the *IV Encontro Inter-
nacional Evoliano* conference in São Paulo, Brazil in September 2014.

supposing the course of history to be the varying manifestations of a developing *Weltgeist*, or world-spirit, whereas Marx's materialist historiography was ruled by mere economic alterations. Nevertheless, the falsehood of even Hegel's philosophy of history is made clear to anyone who considers the history of the country which is actually promoting liberal democracy now as a universal norm: America.

From its inception as an independent nation, in America there has hardly been any deviation from liberal democratic goals, and Communism and Fascism have not only been absent there in their European forms but are, if ever they emerge, quickly absorbed into the nation's unchanging liberal democratic framework. What American society actually represents is a sort of ahistorical, quasi-Communist utopia where private individuals strive ever more strenuously to possess the means of production and to resist the interference of the state in public affairs. There is also little to distinguish the Communist ideal of equality from the liberal. When Fukuyama suggests that we have come to the 'end of history', what he therefore means is that the world that has undergone genuine historical changes has now been conquered by a country that began and continues as a utopia that is as little capable of historical change as of real progress; that is, progress understood not in the technological, but in the traditional sense of the development of the spiritual, intellectual, and social attitudes of a people.

The 'end of history' is indeed a phenomenon that is peculiar to America as a British colony that has had tenuous connections with the naturally developing history of the Old World. While most countries founded by colonial settlement manage to maintain and develop the culture of their mother nation to a certain extent – as Australia, for example, has done – America began and developed at a time of Protestant and Puritan revolt against the ancient Catholic monarchical traditions of Britain. It is therefore important to consider the phenomenon of Puritanism, which provoked the English Civil War at the time that America was being settled, and to notice the close connection between Christian Puritanism and Judaism.

We may recall in this context that the Jews, who had been officially expelled from England in 1290 by Edward I, were allowed by the Puritan dictator Oliver Cromwell in the 1650s to return from Holland, where they had been conducting a flourishing financial business. Throughout the Commonwealth, the Jews were held in high esteem by the Puritans. The similarity of the capitalist ethics developed by the Puritans to that of the Jews was noted in 1911 by the German sociologist Werner Sombart in his work *Die Juden und das Wirtschaftsleben*. Sombart maintained that the 'Protestant' ethic that Max Weber had focussed on in his 1905 work, *Die protestantische Ethik und der Geist des Kapitalismus*, was indeed to be identified specifically as a Puritan one that should be equated with Judaism. For, as Sombart explained,

> In both will be found . . . the close relationship between religion and business, the arithmetical conception of sin, and, above all, the rationalization of life.[2]

With the American Civil War of 1861–65, the last links with monarchical England that had persisted in the pro-English South were cut by the victory of the federalist North. Then, in the aftermath of the Civil War, in the late nineteenth and early twentieth centuries, the Christian religious aspect of the original Puritan work-ethic of the Americans was seriously impaired by the large-scale influx of Jews from central and eastern Europe, who succeeded in modulating the philo-Semitic Puritan character of American capitalism into a fully Jewish one. As Sombart pointed out, the Jews had indeed been active in American economic life already from the seventeenth century, and had gradually come to monopolise many branches of American commerce such as the wheat, tobacco, and cotton trades. But we must note that with the increased immigration of eastern Jews at the end of the nineteenth century and the promotion of Jewish finance capitalism, what remained of the original Puritan work-ethic

---

[2] Sombart, *The Jews and Modern Capitalism*, p. 249.

and concomitant frugality in the American economy was soon dissipated, while the only vestige of the dissident Puritanical religiosity that survived was its stubborn anti-clericalism.

With the replacement of the Puritan veneration of industry by the parasitical reign of finance, the Jewish tendency for economic utopianism which manifested itself in the twentieth century as totalitarian Communism in Russia, eastern Europe, and the Far East was transformed in the new "promised land' of the Jews into the totalitarian liberalism of the 'American Dream'. As Sombart put it, 'what we call Americanism is nothing else, if we may say so, than the Jewish spirit distilled'.[3] The capitalism promoted by the Jews steadily strengthened the nation's commitment to individualistic freedom and material aggrandisement rather than to the civilisational aims of the old monarchies and empires. Naturally, such a nation could not evolve or acquire a human history. Instead of producing examples of human greatness, it could only boast of a bourgeoisie that aspired to millionaire status and, instead of historical development, it could only experience periodic economic booms and recessions.

In his book, Fukuyama himself attempts to introduce a Nietzschean question into his glorification of liberal democracy by raising the spectre of the 'last man', or the average American-like man whose life is materially sated and spiritually meaningless. But with naïve optimism, he maintains that such an intolerably vacuous life will certainly be held at bay in a liberal democracy by man's spiritedness, a human characteristic that will inevitably rebel against such a monotonous existence. This spiritedness is the same as what Plato called the middle part of the tripartite soul, between its rational and animal parts. In the liberal democratic system, in Fukuyama's view, instead of this passionate energy's reappearance in violent strife, as in the case of nationalist or imperialistic states, there will be an absorption of it into sports, business, and political shows – such as election campaigns.

---

[3] *Ibid.*, p. 44.

Fukuyama's belief in the sort of social engineering that liberal democracy universally aims at ignores the vast difference between the states of the Old World and the American. Indeed, the Neoconservative enterprise propagated by Fukuyama serves as a timely reminder of the incompatibility of the American with genuinely European systems of political thought. The American social values that are being imposed on Europe and the rest of the world via economic and military means are essentially alien ones, and are neither likely to take root easily nor endure. This is because, unlike the American nation, European and other older nations have a historical vitality that cannot be suffocated by American avarice. In order to illustrate this fact, I shall survey the characteristic political traditions of the Indo-Europeans and the contradictory intellectual movements that have distorted these traditions in the course of modern history.

II

To understand the traditional Indo-European social ethos, I may begin with the paradigmatic Āryan conception of society discernible in ancient India. The famous 'caste system' of the Indians is, unlike the modern Western 'class system', an entirely spiritual one, and men are recognised not by their economic status but by their hereditary spiritual capacity. The four Indian social orders are represented symbolically as the head, arms, thighs, and feet of the primordial cosmic anthropomorphic form of the divine Soul called Purusha. The manifestation of the Soul itself is understood to occur as a result of its three inherent forms of energy, *sattva, rajas,* and *tamas* – the first representing pure existence, the second motion, and the third inertia.[4] Since there is an intimate and unavoidable correspondence between the macrocosm and the human microcosm, these three energies appear embodied in differing degrees among humans as well. The sattvic element most fully manifests in the brāhmans; the

---

[4] *Brahmānda Purāna,* I,i,3,12.

rājasic in the warriors, or kshatriyas; and the tāmasic in the vaisyas and shudras – particularly the latter. This is the original spiritual and psychological basis of all social hierarchy.

The brāhman owes his preeminent position in society to his superhuman spiritual power. Brahman, the deity who represents the Intellectual light of the cosmos, itself derives from a word denoting creative power, and it is the privilege and duty of the brāhman to represent this creative power. The kshatriyas, or political rulers and warriors, only serve to maintain this creative power, both within the land and also in the universe. The brāhman and kshatriya thus constitute the paradigmatic Indo-European polity centred on the dual organs of what in European politics are called Church and State. The people as such do not have a major political role, either as a bourgeoisie or as a proletariat.

If we turn to the Greek philosophers, we find that in Plato and Aristotle the state is again constantly conceived of in terms of the constitution of the universal and individual soul. According to Plato, the soul is 'that which moves itself'[5] and is naturally prior to the body, since it 'is what governs all the changes and modifications of bodies'.[6]

Just as in ancient India, the soul, or psyche, in Plato's *Republica* (Republic), Book IV, is divided into three parts: a higher rational or spiritual part (called *logistikon*), corresponding to the Indian *sattva*; a middle passionate one (called *thymoeides*), corresponding to *rajas*; and a lower sensual part (called *epithymetikon*), corresponding to *tamas*. Since society is as organic a phenomenon as the individuals of which it is composed, in a state as well the more the rational aspect predominates over the passionate, the closer it approximates to the ideal political form. But the discipline of the lower desires by the dictates of reason is to be found in only a few, and these are the 'best born and the best educated' men,[7] whereas the untrained and untamed passions are to be found in abundance among children, women,

---

[5] Plato, *Phaedrus*, 246a.

[6] Plato, *Laws*, 892a.

[7] Plato, *Republica*, Book IV.

and the lower classes, which form the largest section of society. The aristocratic 'guardians' of Plato's ideal republic are therefore required to be true philosophers, and will not be drawn from the inferior classes.

Aristotle continues Plato's spiritually-oriented political theory in his *Ethica Nichomachea* (Nicomachean Ethics), where he declares that the primary aim of politics is the attainment of the good of the nation. The higher classes of a nation will comprise the full citizens, who will assume the military and administrative – including priestly – offices of the land. The legislators must govern with a clear knowledge of the spiritual constitution of man; that is, the rational and passionate elements that Plato had discerned in the individual soul. And it is the duty of the legislators to ensure the predominance of the higher aspect of the soul over the lower.

Platonic principles reappear in the European Renaissance in the writings of aristocratic thinkers like Francesco Guicciardini and Jean Bodin. According to Guicciardini, who offered a critique of Niccolò Machiavelli in one of his works, *Considerazioni intorno ai 'Discorsi' del Machiavelli sopra la prima deca di Tito Livio* (Considerations on the Discourses of Machiavelli, 1528), the chief reason that a prince and an aristocracy is superior to the people is that they are not subject to pernicious passions, such as – notably – envy. The French Renaissance philosopher Jean Bodin, who is notable for his championing of monarchical absolutism, also based his defence of the latter on a similar Platonic basis. Genuine monarchy is, according to him, derived from the Divine Law, and the monarch is the earthly image of God. Care should be taken that the religious foundation of the state is never brought into doubt, and religious leaders must act as censors of the state in order to maintain moral discipline within it.

It is at this juncture in world history that the revolutionary anti-monarchical ideas of the English Civil War, the American Revolution, and the French Revolution appear. If we study the American Bill of Rights of 1789, we realise that it was based largely on the English Bill of Rights of 1689 promulgated by the (originally Puritan) English Parliament after the 'Glorious' Protestant Revolution of 1688 in order to curb the powers traditionally invested in the formerly Catholic monarchs of England. One of the most influential English thinkers of the seventeenth century – and one generally considered to be the father of liberal democracy – was John Locke, who was also a Puritan. Locke was a champion of the separation of the Church and State, and had a profound influence on the American 'Founding Fathers' such as Thomas Jefferson. The American Bill of Rights, based on the British parliamentarian one, is especially notable for its dissociation (in the First Amendment) of the American state from any official religion. What had begun in England as a rejection of Catholicism was thus turned into a rejection of all official religion in America. Combined with this fear of theocracy was the Puritanical devotion to individual freedom and industry which caused the Americans to view citizenship as a status defined primarily by liberty, and citizens as economic units of production not unlike those of the later Communist utopia of Marx.

A little later, in the middle of the eighteenth century, Jean-Jacques Rousseau propagated the Lockean conception of government in France as a social 'contract' directed by the *volonté générale* of the people, which would reduce the inequalities springing from subservience to the state. However, a robust answer to Rousseau's doctrine of the 'social contract' was offered immediately after the fateful French Revolution by the English political philosopher Edmund Burke in his *Reflections on the Revolution in France* (1790), where he pointed out that

> the state ought not to be considered as nothing better than a partnership agreement in a trade of pepper and coffee, calico or tobacco, or some such low concern . . .[8]

And since the people cannot be relied upon to follow any 'general will' towards the attainment of the good of the nation, Burke

---

[8] Edmund Burke, *Reflections on the Revolution in France*, in *The Works of Edmund Burke* (Boston: Charles C. Little & James Brown, 1839), Chapter III, p. 120.

proposed a natural aristocracy as the only viable national government. A strong nation is also necessarily a religious one for, as Burke said, all politicians indeed act on behalf of 'the one great Master, Author and Founder of society',[9] namely God. Religion's vital role in the conduct of states was reiterated in post-revolutionary France by the French monarchist Count Joseph de Maistre as well, who noted in his *Essai sur le principes générateur des constitutions politiques et des autres institutions humaines* (Essay on the Generating Principle of Political Constitutions and Other Human Institutions, 1809) that 'the duration of empires has always been proportionate to the degree of influence the religious element gained in the political constitution'.[10] Indeed, the truly political laws of a land are synonymous with the religious feelings of the people and the 'instant [man] separates himself from God to act alone . . . he does not lose power . . . but his activity is negative and leads only to destruction'.[11] To follow the doctrines of Enlightenment thinkers like Rousseau and Voltaire would thus result in a return to a state of anarchy and degeneracy.

In Germany around the same time, philosophers like Immanuel Kant and Johann Gottlieb Fichte were beginning to point to the crucial significance of the 'state' as the means of enforcing an enlightened government. Kant took as his point of departure the excellence of Divine Law in relation to Natural Law, so that Reason, or the Moral Law, was elevated far above the mindless workings of Nature. To establish this rule of the Moral Law on earth, Kant proposed a supremely powerful state that would control all religious and commercial offices in the land.

The leader of the state can never be a democratic representative of the people since democracy inevitably results in despotism. While Kant favoured a monarchical republic, Fichte advocated a Platonic philosopher-statesman who is at once a political

---

[9] *Ibid.*, p. 116.

[10] 'Essay' in Joseph de Maistre, *On God and Society*, tr. E. Greifer (Chicago: H. Regnery Co., 1959), p. 42.

[11] *Ibid.*, p. 63.

and religious leader of his nation. Like a Platonic 'guardian', such a statesman

> in his estimate of mankind looks beyond that which they are in the actual world to that which they are in the Divine Idea . . .[12]

The monarch will bear the responsibility for the realisation of the inner freedom of the individuals within his nation. It is important to note in this context Fichte's emphasis that the aim of all society is 'ever-increasing ennoblement of the human race, that is, to set it more and more at liberty from the bondage of Nature',[13] just as the aim of all culture is 'to subject Nature . . . to Reason'.[14] In order to counteract the spurious freedom that the young in particular hanker after, Fichte insists that a new system of education must be developed which 'essentially destroys the freedom of will . . . and produces on the contrary strict necessity in the decisions of the will'.[15]

The state continues to be glorified in Hegel's Idealistic philosophy. For Hegel the state – and especially the Prussian state – is the 'embodiment of rational freedom realising and recognising itself in an objective form'.[16] And in the Prussian nationalism of Heinrich von Treitschke, the state is glorified to an extent that it becomes a sort of substitute for God. Treitschke takes care to stress that 'the consciousness of national unity is dependent on a common bond of religion, for religious sentiment is one of the fundamental forces of the

---

[12] 'The Nature of the Scholar', in *The Popular Works of Johann Gottlieb Fichte*, tr. W. Smith (London: J. Chapman, 1848), Vol. I, p. 290.

[13] 'The Vocation of the Scholar', *loc. cit.*, p. 180.

[14] *Ibid.*, p. 175.

[15] *Addresses to the German Nation*, tr. R. F. Jones & G. H. Turnbull (Chicago: Open Court Publishing Co., 1922), p. 20.

[16] *Lectures on the Philosophy of History*, tr. J. Sibree (London: George Bell and & Sons, 1881), p. 49.

human character'.[17] Unfortunately, the interference of Jewish elements in German politics had disturbed the traditional spiritual ordering of society by encouraging 'the coexistence of several religions within one nationality, involving an irreconcilable and ultimately intolerable difference of outlook upon life'.[18]

Directly opposed to these several statist doctrines of the German Idealists and nationalists is the doctrine of Communism, which was propounded in the middle of the nineteenth century by the Jewish political economist Karl Marx. The radical difference between the Marxist view of the world and the Indo-European is already evident in the fact that Marx's system was based on a materialism that totally denied the existence of any spiritual reality whatsoever, and all metaphysics in general, in favour of a dialectical socio-economics that attempted to understand the transformations of society according to its changing modes of production. Unlike Hegel, who had justified history as the changing manifestations of a quasi-divine world-spirit, Marx wished to 'create' history by focussing on what he considered its essential economic activities. As he put it in *The German Ideology*:

> Morality, religion, metaphysics, all the rest of ideology and their corresponding forms of consciousness . . . have no history, no development; but men, developing their material production and their material intercourse, alter, along with their real existence, their thinking and the products of their thinking.[19]

However, the Communist system, for all its apparent evolutionary aspirations, is an anti-scientific, utopian construct aiming at an anti-human classless and stateless society based on the

---

[17] Heinrich von Treitschke, *Politics*, Vol. I, tr. A. J. Balfour (NY: Macmillan Co., 1916), p. 53.

[18] *Ibid.*, Vol. I, p. 334.

[19] Karl Marx, *The German Ideology*, ed. C. J. Arthur (New York: International Publishers, 1970), p. 47.

common ownership of the means of production. In this de-lusional sociological experiment, Marx focused especially on class-struggle, or the conflict between capital and labour, as the primary instrument of historical change. By granting economic, social, and political equality to all citizens, Marx believed that the social awareness and discipline of every individual would naturally be increased. And, while he tolerated a representative parliamentary political system as a transitional stage, his Communist utopia aimed at a final dissolution of the state apparatus (which is what induces hierarchy and inequality) at the most advanced state of Communism, when the people would become fully self-governing.

Marxism is thus the fullest expression of a liberal world-view that is diametrically opposed to the traditional or conservative Indo-European ordering of society according to spiritual character which we have observed in ancient India, Greece, and the rest of Europe until the advent of Puritanism in the middle of the seventeenth century. Marxism is naturally also opposed to the state structure that supports the religious and warrior aris-tocracy that founded, constitutes, and preserves the nation. It may be noted here that, although modern liberal democracies pretend to abhor the Communist ideology, the arrogation of political powers in the West by the commercial middle class represents a major step towards the same dissolution of the concepts of national authority and sovereignty that Communism, too, strives for.

III

Marx's political economic theories were strongly criticised at the turn of the century by many notable German thinkers like Eugen Dühring and Oswald Spengler, but I should like to highlight here two of the most metaphysically structured political philosophical responses to Marxism – namely, the theories of the Italian Fascist philosopher Giovanni Gentile and the pro-Fascist thinker Julius Evola.

According to Gentile, the basis of evil, exactly as in Plato and Plotinus, is matter, or nature, which is opposed to spirit and represents as it were

> not merely moral and absolute nullity [but] the impenetrable chaos of brute nature, mechanism, spiritual darkness, falsehood and evil, all the things that man is forever fighting against.[20]

Gentile points out that the economic life focussed on by Marx is marked by a utilitarianism akin to the instinctual life of animals and is a life of slavery to matter, whereas politics should be a means to spiritual freedom. Indeed, Marxism aimed at the worst sort of social organisation, 'the utilitarian, materialistic and hence egoistic conception of life understood as a realm of rights to be vindicated, instead of as an arena of duties to be performed by sacrificing oneself to an ideal'.[21] On the other hand, the Fascist understands life as being

> serious, austere, religious; entirely balanced in a world sustained by the moral and responsible forces of the spirit. The Fascist disdains the 'easy life'.[22]

Gentile's understanding of society is based on a Kantian ideal of a 'transcendent society', which is produced by the interaction of the ego and its pure object, the alter ego. It is this conception of a 'transcendent society' which makes man a 'political animal', as Aristotle had suggested. The gradual self-realisation of an individual necessarily entails the enlightenment of his objective counterparts, the other members of society, so that the nation

---

[20] Giovanni Gentile, *Genesis and Structure of Society*, tr. H. S. Harris (Urbana, IL: University of Illinois Press, 1946), p. 120.

[21] 'What is Fascism?', in H. W. Schneider, *Making the Fascist State* (NY: Howard Fertig, 1968), p. 350.

[22] 'Fundamental Ideas', in Benito Mussolini, *The Doctrine of Fascism*, tr. I. S. Munro, in *Readings on Fascism and National Socialism*, ed. A. Swallow (Columbus, OH: Swallow Press, 1984).

as a whole begins to approach the ideal 'transcendent society'.

For Gentile, as for Fichte, the proper intellectual activity of the enlightened individual is the comprehension of the whole of mankind – or of the Idea of it. And the 'state' is the objective embodiment of the personality of the individuals constituting it, or the 'universal common aspect' of their will. As he explained in the introductory essay, 'Fundamental Ideas', to Benito Mussolini's *Dottrina politica e sociale del fascismo* (The Political and Social Doctrine of Fascism), the state stands for 'the universal conscience and will of man in his historic existence'.[23] True political liberty is therefore possible only when the individuals that constitute the state become free through the realisation of the universal aspect of their personality.

The state in its universal aspect is indeed an image of the Divine Will, and the laws of the State must ever be in consonance with the Divine Law. Religion, naturally, is not an external aid to the will of the state, but its constitutive element. As he explained in 'Fundamental Ideas':

> Fascism is a religious conception in which man is considered to be in the powerful grip of a superior law, with an objective will which transcends the particular individual and elevates him into a fully conscious member of a spiritual society.[24]

The prime task of the state is to foster the dual development of individuals and of the society. As he put it, the Fascist state

> reassumes all the forms of the moral and intellectual life of man. It cannot, therefore, be limited to a simple function of order and of safeguarding, as was contended by Liberalism. It is not a simple mechanism which limits the sphere of the presumed individual liberties. It is an internal form and rule, a discipline of the entire person: it penetrates the will as well as the intelligence. Its principle, a central inspiration of the living human personality in the civil community, descends into the

---

[23] *Ibid.*

[24] *Ibid.*

depths and settles in the heart of the man of action as well as the thinker, of the artist as well as of the scientist . . .[25]

Thus,

> Fascism would . . . not be understood in many of its manifestations (as, for example, in its organisations of the Party, its system of education, its discipline) were it not considered in the light of its general view of life. A spiritualised view.
>
> To Fascism the world is not this material world which appears on the surface, in which man is an individual separated from all other men, standing by himself and subject to a natural law which instinctively impels him to lead a life of momentary and egoistic pleasure. In Fascism man is an individual who is the nation and the country. He is this by a moral law which embraces and binds together individuals and generations in an established tradition and mission, a moral law which suppresses the instinct to lead a life confined to a brief cycle of pleasure in order, instead, to replace it within the orbit of duty in a superior conception of life, free from the limits of time and space, a life in which the individual by self-abnegation and by the sacrifice of his particular interests, even by death, realises the entirely spiritual existence in which his value as a man consists.[26]

For the Fascist views on the formation of an elite or aristocracy in a modern state, we may rely on the views of the other Italian thinker, Julius Evola, whose commentaries on Fascist Italy and National Socialist Germany contain invaluable counsels on statecraft.[27] Though Evola criticised Gentile for what he considered to be the moralist aspect of Gentile's state, both thinkers place an equal emphasis on the transcendental dimension of the state. Evola notes this aspect especially in the Fascist

---

[25] *Ibid.*

[26] *Ibid.*

[27] See Julius Evola, *Fascism Viewed from the Right*, tr. E. Christian Kopff (London: Arktos, 2013), and *Notes on the Third Reich*, tr. E. Christian Kopff (London: Arktos, 2013).

conception of the state rather than in the National Socialist one:

> in Fascist political doctrine . . . [t]he state was recognised as possessing pre-eminence in respect to people and nation, that is, the dignity of a single superior power through which the nation acquires a real self-awareness, possesses a form and a will, and participates in a supernatural order.[28]

As Gentile had stated,

> the nation does not beget the State, according to the decrepit nationalistic concept which was used as a basis for the publicists of the national States in the nineteenth century. On the contrary, the nation is created by the State, which gives the people, conscious of their own moral unity, the will, and thereby an effective existence.[29]

In National Socialist Germany, on the other hand, the racial nation took precedence over the state, which had in fact been represented earlier by the Prussian state of the Hohenzollerns:

> . . . Prussia had been the creation of a dynasty that had the nobility, the army and the higher bureaucracy for its backbone. The primary element was not the 'nation' or the *Volk*. Rather the state, more than the land or the ethnos, constituted the real foundation and unifying principle. There was none of that in Hitlerism – at least in the area of general political ideology. The state was conceived as a secondary and instrumental reality, while the primary formative, moving and bearing force was supposed to be the *Volk* with the *Führer* as its representative and incarnation.[30]

A populist state is in fact a counterfeit version of the Fascist state, since it is a 'mass state' characterised by

---

[28] *Fascism Vewed from the Right*, p. 32.

[29] Gentile, 'Fundamental Ideas', *loc. cit.*

[30] Evola, *Notes on the Third Reich*, p. 37.

collectivising and demagogic movements with an excitable and sub-rational foundation, which can also give to the individual the illusory, momentary sensation of an exalted, intense life, likewise conditioned by sensation, by a regression, and by a reduction of personality and true liberty.[31]

Evola aptly cites the German writer Ernst von Salomon (1902–1972) in order to show that populist nationalism is incompatible with a conservative political one:

There could not be, from the historical point of view, any bridge between the state idea and the populist one of the essence of the nation. This fact, unfortunately, was disguised by the disorienting circumstance that the populist formula used the same vocabulary and boasted of being a renewed conception of the state.[32]

Not having a strong notion of the state, the Third Reich was also incapable of establishing a supra-national state structure such as the Habsburg Empire pre-eminently had done. The National Socialist slogan of 'Ein Reich, ein Volk, ein Führer' was perhaps adequate for pan-Germanist aims, but not for a pan-European one. This inadequacy was especially compounded by the doctrines of Nordic supremacy that made enemies of fellow European nations – such as the Poles, most notably – that could have been turned instead into allies against the Communist state.

That the state is distinct from the nation and the *Gemeinschaft* (the 'community' of Ferdinand Tönnies) does not mean that it is identical to the *Gesellschaft* (society), either. In fact, Evola clearly identifies the societal focus of liberal political theory as its greatest defect:

In reality, there is a fundamental antithesis of doctrine between political systems that focus on the idea of the state

---

[31] Evola, *Fascism Viewed from the Right*, p. 48.

[32] *Ibid.*, p. 39.

and those that focus on the idea of 'society' (the 'social' type of state). The second type of system includes the varieties of theories based upon the concept of natural rights, contract theory with a utilitarian base, and democracy, with the related developments that stretch from liberal democracy to the so-called 'people's democracies', that is, Marxist and Communist ones.[33]

A Fascist state, on the other hand, is concerned with the 'transcendence' that can be achieved only through heroic or military virtues such as 'honour and loyalty' that are 'not only beyond hedonistic values (those of simple material well-being), but also eudemonistic ones (that is, ones including spiritual well-being)'. Evola goes on to add that even

> [i]f it is not possible to ask everyone to follow an 'ascetic and military vision of life', it will be possible to aim at a climate of concentrated intensity, of personal life, that will encourage people to prefer a greater margin of liberty, as opposed to comfort and prosperity . . .[34]

The Fascist state, as an organic rather than a mechanical creation, is centralised, but not totalitarian, and allows individual liberty except 'when it is necessary to rein in a shapeless and atomistic mass of individuals and wills'.[35] In a Fascist state, which is directed against both capitalism and Communism, the centre will be constituted of a principle of authority and a transcendent symbol of sovereignty. The most natural incarnation of such a symbol is the monarchy. However,

> [m]onarchy is not incompatible with a 'legal dictatorship', more or less as it was in ancient Roman law. The sovereign can confer exceptional unitary powers on a person of special stature and qualification, still on a legal basis, when there

---

[33] *Ibid.*, p. 35.

[34] *Ibid.*, p. 121.

[35] *Ibid.*, p. 42.

are special situations to overcome or exceptional tasks to confront.[36]

Thus, when lacking an effective monarch (*rex*), a state can substitute a 'dictator' (*dux*), who however acts 'by the legitimate and pre-existing system of order, essentially destined to integrate it in case of necessity' in order to consolidate 'a particular concentration and activation of existing forces'.[37] This leader, too, cannot be a modern 'man of the people' (as in the case of National Socialism or Communism, or in the present American presidential system), where

> People only put up with the leader who is, essentially, 'one of us', who is 'one of the people', who expresses the 'will of the people', who is a 'good friend'.[38]

The democratic system of endlessly fluctuating party politics is to be firmly rejected even though the parliamentary framework may be retained – albeit in a higher aristocratic form. That is, the upper parliamentary house, or the House of Lords, should serve as the essential government of the nation and be constituted of an elite that corresponds to the ancient Indo-European offices of the priest and the warrior. This elite,

> by inserting itself into the normal and essential hierarchies of the state and eventually controlling it, . . . bears, to an eminent degree, the idea [of the state]. In this last case, more than a 'party' it will be appropriate to speak of a kind of 'order'. This is the same function that in other times was exercised by the nobility as a political class . . .[39]

Though representing the nobility in the modern world, the elite occupying the upper House of Parliament 'will also act as the

---

[36] *Ibid.*, p. 118.

[37] *Ibid.*, p. 47.

[38] *Ibid.*, p. 63.

[39] *Ibid.*, p. 58.

guardian of the idea of the state, and will prevent the "caesarean" isolation of whoever exercises the supreme authority".[40]

The Lower House of Parliament should be constituted not of parties that have gained entrance through the weight of popular votes, but of corporate 'bodies', including the several economic ones, which are all characterised by their 'function and dignity'. Just as the Upper House will serve as an advisory council to the King or President, the Lower will work in coordination with the ministers and the Prime Minister.

The task of the Upper House is first of all to establish its control over the economic powers of the land that are vested primarily in the middle class:

> The sphere of politics and power should be, by its very nature and function, free from economic influences, influences by economic groups or special interests. It is appropriate to recall the statement of Sulla, who said that his ambition was not to possess gold, but to hold power over those who possess it.[41]

This hierarchical constitution of the Parliament will preclude the domination of the interests of the lower orders, including the bourgeois ones. As Evola points out, a Fascist state should take care

> [o]n the one hand, . . . to eliminate the proletarian and Marxist influences on the worker, and on the other to destroy the purely 'capitalist' mentality of the entrepreneur.[42]

In general, what Evola desires is a total reformation of industrial society in a heroic/military fashion

> against the Marxist and materialist mentality, the same type of 'military' attitude in the general sense, of which we have

---

[40] *Ibid.*, p. 119.

[41] *Ibid.*, p. 120.

[42] *Ibid.*, p. 80.

spoken earlier, could be made equally effective on the level of work and production.[43]

The urgent task of restoring the primacy of politics over economics can be achieved through strictly controlling 'the monstrous development of capitalism in the direction of unfettered productivity' so that it is

> limited, with the ultimate end of restoring the economy, and everything that is economic, to the subordinate position in which it becomes only a means to an end, and a circumscribed dominion within a much vaster hierarchy of values and interests.[44]

Industry's craving for unlimited change should be reined in by the state so as to allow

> progress or movement in a 'vertical' direction, for the realisation of higher possibilities and the true autonomy of the person . . .[45]

The aim of the Fascist state should indeed be the Stoic ideal of 'autarky', or

> an ethics of independence or the sovereignty of the individual. In order to guard this value, where it was necessary, one had to follow the strict principle of *abstine et sustine*.[46]

The national economy, too, should be marked by 'austerity' in the sense of

> if necessary, holding the general standard of living relatively low, adopting what the English call 'austerity', which, even

---

[43] *Ibid.*, p. 81.

[44] *Ibid.*, p. 91.

45 *Ibid.*, p. 92.

[46] *Ibid.*, p. 88 (Latin: 'abstain and sustain').

119

in a different context, has had to be practiced here and there by different nations after the Second World War, but assuring ourselves a maximum of independence.[47]

Thus, as regards the life of the nation in general,

> we hold the normal situation to be the complete opposite of everything we are witnessing today: apparently generalised prosperity and thoughtless living from day to day beyond one's means, along with a frightening state debt balance, leading to extreme economic and social instability, growing inflation and an invasion of foreign capital which brings with it many important visible and invisible influences.[48]

Only a state pitched at the level of spiritual 'transcendence' can foster 'the development of personality and true liberty in the sense of *virtus*,[49] according to the Classical understanding'.[50] As Evola explains,

> [i]n truth, personality and liberty can be conceived only on the basis of the individual's freeing himself, to a certain degree, from the naturalistic, biological and primitively individualist bonds that characterise the pre-state and pre-political forms [directed] in a purely social, utilitarian and contractual sense.[51]

In these Fascist conceptions of history and of the philosophical significance of the state we see thus the diametrical opposite of the liberal American way of life. They, further, provide a powerful corrective to the historiographical errors of Hegelians like Fukuyama who raise the political *status quo* to an ideal after superficially surveying the external changes of a state, as also to

---

[47] *Ibid.*

[48] *Ibid.*

[49] Latin: 'manly virtue'.

[50] *Ibid.*, pp. 47-48.

[51] *Ibid.*, p. 47.

the errors of the Marxists who conjure up utopias from these same changes. All of these thinkers ignore the transcendent or divine aspect of statecraft, which, as we have observed in our initial survey of ancient Indian and Greek philosophy, also provides the true basis of the necessary hierarchical organisation of society. The state should ever bear in mind the constitution of the psyche or soul itself and aim, through a sacred kingship or an enlightened aristocracy, at the psychological improvement of the individuals that comprise the state.

Materialistic societies governed by economically oriented political doctrines, whether Puritan, Marxist, or capitalist, are incapable of any real historical development because the spiritual element of man – which alone is capable of movement and development – is not best tended by either the middle or the lower classes, but only by an upper class constituted of what the British aptly call the 'lords spiritual and temporal'. Fukuyama's historiographic thesis is thus merely a description of the abortive state of America itself, which has through its history gradually substituted materialistic and economic principles of statecraft for the spiritual ones that originally governed all European monarchies, including the British.

In considering this American problem, we cannot afford to ignore the fateful role that the Jewish bourgeoisie have played in the history of the West, for the re-entry of the Jews into England during the Puritan revolution is psychologically linked to the capitalist career of the new American state, as well as to its inevitable transformation into a bourgeois oligarchy. Indeed, all modern political theories that aim at a diminution or dissolution of the state or of the leading religious institution of a nation, whether these theories are called libertarian, populist, or anarchist, may be recognised as derivatives of the defective Jewish economic mentality, which is also responsible for the social degeneration generally associated with modernism.

This mentality can, and should, be fully replaced by genuinely Indo-European political doctrines that are not enunciated by the bourgeoisie in the name of the people, but by the non-mercantile, aristocratic section of the population that alone can serve as the leaders of a cultured state. Politically, the alliance of both the state and its leading religious institution – in the West's case, the Church – must be consolidated and their role strengthened through the Upper House of the Parliament. The current parliamentary structure of government should be reorganised so that the economic concerns of the Lower House and of the Prime Minister's cabinet are dominated by the more aristocratic ones of an Upper House dedicated to the elevation of the idea of the state and its people. This will naturally mean the exclusion of all anti-statist and bourgeois elements – including the Jewish – from the higher echelons of government and society.

The philosophical guidelines for the regeneration of nations are already to be found in the long tradition of European conservative philosophy that I have surveyed, and that come to a sharp focus in the Fascist doctrines of Gentile and Evola. Of course, Fascism – lazily conflated with National Socialism – has today become a term that is abhorrent to those who blindly follow Judaised America in its various utopian adventures. But it is well to bear in mind that the price of American utopianism is the end of history.

Appendix

Hannah Arendt and the Zionist Question[1]

Hannah Arendt (1906–1975), the German-Jewish thinker who emigrated to America from Germany in the middle of the last century, is well-known for her studies of *The Origins of Totalitarianism* (1951, with three sections on 'Antisemitism', 'Imperialism' and 'Totalitarianism'), *The Human Condition* (1958), and her work on the American and French revolutions, *On Revolution* (1963). Arendt had studied under Martin Heidegger in Marburg, under Edmund Husserl in Freiburg, and Karl Jaspers in Heidelberg before she was forced to leave Germany for France in 1933. After her flight from Germany, she lived in Paris until 1941, when she emigrated to the United States.

Arendt's opposition to totalitarianism and sympathy for socialism led her to advocate for political activism in support of individual human freedom. Her various sociological works were influenced not only by her studies in existential philosophy, but also by the sociology of Max Weber, whose

---

[1] This essay was published as 'Hannah Arendt on the Jews and the Jewish State' in *Counter-Currents*, April 11, 2019 (www.counter-currents.com/2019/04/hannah-arendt-on-the-jews-the-jewish-state/).

appellation of Jewry as a 'pariah people' in his book *Wirtschaft und Gesellschaft* (Economy and Society, 1921),[2] influenced her own conception of the identity of the Jewish people in European society. Her views on the Jewish Question expressed in essays written in the thirties, forties, fifties, and sixties and collected in *The Jewish Writings* by Jerome Kohn and Ron. H. Feldman[3] are particularly interesting for the glimpse they provide into the mentality of the assimilated and educated Jews of Germany in the first half of the twentieth century.

Assimilation and Anti-Semitism

Arendt's preferred Jewish society within Europe was that of the early nineteenth century, when Berlin's Jewish salons had become home to aristocrats and artists, both of whom were outside the bourgeoisie, just as the Jews, as 'pariahs', were as well.[4] The Berlin salon of Rahel Varnhagen (1771–1833), for example, provided a meeting place for artists, poets, and intellectuals such as Friedrich Schlegel, Friedrich Schelling, Friedrich Schleiermacher, Alexander and Wilhelm von Humboldt, Friedrich de la Motte Fouqué, Ludwig Tieck, Jean Paul, and Friedrich Gentz.[5] Though Arendt does not remark on this fact, these figures of the Romantic movement who attended

---

[2] Max Weber, *Wirtschaft und Gesellschaft: Grundriss der verstehenden Soziologie* (Tübingen: J. C. B. Mohr, 1921); English edition: *On Law and Economy in Society*, tr. Max Rheinstein (Cambridge, MA: Harvard University Press, 1954).

[3] Hannah Arendt, *The Jewish Writings*, ed. J. Kohn and R. H. Feldman (NY: Schocken Books, 2007).

[4] See Arendt, 'Antisemitism', in *op.cit.*

[5] Arendt was an ardent admirer of Varnhagen and wrote a biography of her in 1938 which was published in 1957 as *Rahel Varnhagen: Lebensgeschichte einer deutschen Jüdin aus der Romantik*. The English translation, by R. and C. Winston, was published as *Rahel Varnhagen: The Life of a Jewess* (Baltimore, MD: Johns Hopkins University Press, 1997).

her salons indeed represented in their works the newly-blossoming bourgeois world of the nineteenth century.[6]

Arendt sympathised particularly with those assimilated Jews of that time who were conscious of their 'pariah' status within Christian European society. She criticised the unthinking assimilationists who gradually withdrew their support for the princely states of Europe and worked for their dissolution. This change was indeed a major source of the increasing anti-Semitism in Europe, and was especially traceable to the 'parvenus' who had favoured total assimilation. She preferred instead those who chose to remain 'pariah Jews' within European society:

> Modern Jewish history, having started with court Jews and continuing with Jewish millionaires and philanthropists, is apt to forget about this other thread of Jewish tradition – the tradition of Heine, Rahel Varnhagen, Sholom Aleichem, of Bernard Lazare, Franz Kafka, or even Charlie Chaplin [sic]. It is the tradition of a minority of Jews who have not wanted to become upstarts, who preferred the status of "conscious pariah." All vaunted Jewish qualities – the "Jewish heart," humanity, humor, disinterested intelligence – are pariah qualities. All Jewish shortcomings – tactlessness, political stupidity, inferiority complexes, and money-grubbing – are characteristic of upstarts. There have always been Jews who did not think it worthwhile to change their humane attitude and their natural insight into reality for the narrowness of caste spirit or the essential unreality of financial transactions.[7]

Here Arendt employs a Heinrich Heine's Rousseauistic distinction between the pariah and the parvenu:

> Confronted with the natural order of things, in which all is equally good, the fabricated order of society, with its manifold classes and ranks, must appear a comic, hopeless attempt of creation to throw down the gauntlet to its

---

[6] See below p. 127.

[7] 'We Refugees', in *Jewish Writings*, p. 274.

creator. It is no longer the outcast pariah who appears the schlemiel, but those who live in the ordered ranks of society and who have exchanged the generous gifts of nature for the idols of social privilege and prejudice. Especially is this true of the parvenu, who was not even born to the system, but chose it of his own free will, and who is called upon to pay the cost meticulously and exactly, whereas others can take things in their stride.[8]

Unlike Karl Marx, who had maintained that the Jews were rootless because they had been chiefly relegated to financial activities in their diaspora, Arendt attributed their increasingly cosmopolitan character to their diminishing financial and political support for states that were beginning to lose their traditional power in Europe. She observes that Jews had originally backed the European princely states as their financiers and participated willingly in the initial phases of assimilation into European society.[9] However, the Jewish bankers had built up the European states to a point where the latter lost their own power. Arendt notes that Jews themselves gradually abandoned their favoured banking jobs for industrial and intellectual ones. They thereby spread international cultural fashions that branded them as leaders of cosmopolitan worldviews.[10]

After the disintegration of the princely states, the Jews continued to function as international bankers, such as the Rothschilds most notably, and gradually created the expanding banking capitalism of the nineteenth century. The court Jew was now being gradually replaced by the rising bourgeois Jew.

The Junkers also turned against the contemporary state when

---

[8] 'The Jew as Pariah', *ibid.*, p. 279.

[9] See her unpublished essay 'Antisemitism', in *op. cit.*

[10] This internationalism among the intelligentsia was studied by the French nationalist Charles Maurras in his essay on 'The Future of the Intelligentsia' as one of the principal vices of the nineteenth century (see Charles Maurras, *'The Future of the Intelligentsia' and 'For a French Awakening'*, tr. Alexander Jacob [London: Arktos, 2016)].

they suffered loss of land due to their arbitrary sale by the monarch. They saw that the Jewish bankers had helped the monarchical distribution of Junker land through their championing of free trade laws that allowed such distribution. In general, the Junkers wished to keep the rising bourgeoisie down and focused on the Jews as the driving force of the latter. When the Junkers finally obtained concessions through the Compensation Act of 1821, they were at the same time forced to accept power only through capitalist means, and thus to assume a pseudo-bourgeois status.[11] With the rise of capitalist oligarchs, these aristocrats joined the petty bourgeois and the guilds in their agitation against bourgeois reforms – and against the Jewish emancipation as well. The Junkers used Christianity as an ally against the Jews and renewed the anti-Semitism of the state to the extent that the Jewish emancipation was repealed in 1823.

The German bourgeoisie, who were generally opposed to the state, were against the aristocrats and the court Jews equally.[12] New 'aristocratic' Statist theories were propounded by conservative thinkers like Adam Müller and Joseph Goerres, who wished to free the state from Jewish financial control. However, the Junkers' propaganda against the 'Jewish' bourgeoisie was so insistent that the German bourgeois themselves soon sought to dissociate themselves from the Jewish bourgeois in order to avoid the stigma that had become attached to their social status. The argumentation of the new rising anti-Semitism was increasingly like that of the original feudal anti-Semitism of Europe. Thus it was that the Junkers were able to export it easily to the east, where the social conditions were still relatively feudal. The peasantry, who were totally neglected in all these processes, formed a natural breeding ground for anti-Semitism.

---

[11] 'Antisemitism', in *op. cit.*, p.105.

[12] For example, Eugen Dühring was opposed to the Junkers as well as the Jews as exploitative sections of society (see my edition of this work, Eugen Dühring, *The Jewish Question as a Racial, Moral and Cultural Question, with a World-Historical Answer*, [London: Ostara Publications, 2017]).

While the growing industrialisation of the nineteenth century encouraged anti-statist sentiment, along with anti-Semitism, the European nation-state was, according to Arendt, further disintegrated in the early twentieth century by National Socialism's collectivist tendencies among Europe's populations.

***

The steady increase in anti-Semitism in the latter part of the nineteenth century gave rise to a desire among some Jewish activists, such as principally Theodor Herzl (1860–1904), for the establishment of a Jewish homeland. In the late nineteenth century, the Dreyfus affair heightened the tension between Jews and Europeans. And Herzl's personal experience of anti-Semitism in Vienna strengthened his belief in Zionism as a solution to the Jewish people in Europe's problems. He was further spurred in his Zionist efforts by the anti-Semitism of European agitators like Adolf Stoecker and Hermann Ahlwardt in Germany, Georg Ritter von Schoenerer and Karl Lueger in Austria, and Édouard Drumont and Paul Déroulède in France. Indeed, he came to believe that anti-Semitism was a universal phenomenon. According to Arendt, Herzl thus adopted a view of reality

> as an eternal, unchanging hostile structure – all goyim everlastingly against all Jews – made the identification of hard-boiledness with realism plausible because it rendered any empirical analysis of actual political factors seemingly superfluous.[13]

However, Herzl did not fully address the question of anti-Semitism *per se,* especially the reasons for it. It was, according to Arendt, Wilhelm Marr (1819–1904), the author of *Der Sieg des Judenthums über das Germanenthum* (The Triumph of Judaism over Germanism, 1879),[14] who first discussed it.

---

[13] 'The Jewish State', in *op. cit.*, p. 384.

[14] Wilhelm Marr, *Der Sieg des Judenthums über das Germanenthum*

Of course, Eugen Dühring (1833–1921) and Werner Sombart (1863–1941) came soon after. Dühring in particular made it clear in his treatise on the Jews, *Die Judenfrage als Racen-, Sitten- und Culturfrage mit einer weltgeschichtlichen Antwort* (The Jewish Question as a Racial, Moral and Cultural Question, 1881),[15] that the Jewish question was one based not on religion, but on the innate character of the Jewish branch of the Semitic race.[16]

Herzl's idea of a Jewish homeland was mostly opposed by the wealthy assimilated Jews, just as it gained a more sympathetic response from eastern European socialist Jews. Baron Moritz von Hirsch and Baron Nathan Rothschild, for example, refused to proffer any aid for Herzl's plan. The people who supported Zionism were largely assimilated bourgeois Jews who were alarmed by the dangers posed by rising anti-Semitism:

> Zionism, hence, was destined primarily, in Western and Central Europe, to offer a solution to these men who were more assimilated than any other class of Jewry and certainly more imbued with European education and cultural values than their opponents. Precisely because they were assimilated enough to understand the structure of the modern national state, they realized the political actuality of antisemitism even if they failed to analyze it, and they wanted the same body politic for the Jewish people.[17]

Pogroms in the 1880s in Russia also caused eastern Jews to move westwards and come into closer cooperation with them. There gradually arose a new 'Sabbatai Zevi' feeling of Jewish

---

(Berlin: Rudolph Costenoble, 1879).

[15] Eugen Dühring, *Die Judenfrage als Racen-, Sitten- und Culturfrage mit einer weltgeschichtlichen Antwort* (Karlsuhe: H. Reuther, 1881).

[16] 'The Jews are, on the other hand, the most vicious minting of the entire Semitic race into a nationality especially dangerous to nations' (Dühring, *The Jewish Question*, p. 47).

[17] 'Zionism Reconsidered', in *op. cit.*, p. 357.

nationalism[18] that united Jewry in their desire for a homeland of their own.

Arendt herself adopted Zionism as the Jewish counterpart of European statist philosophy. However, she was particularly a socialist Zionist, and favoured the socialist political activism of the French journalist Bernard Lazare (1865–1903) – who had also experienced the anti-Semitism associated with the Dreyfus affair – to Herzl's. As Arendt explains:

> In a rather summary way it may be asserted that the Zionist movement was fathered by two typical nineteenth-century European political ideologies, socialism and nationalism. The amalgam of these two seemingly contradictory doctrines was generally effected long before Zionism came into being: it was effected in all those national revolutionary movements of small European peoples whose situation was equally one of social as of national oppression. But within the Zionist movement such an amalgam has never been realized. Instead, the movement was split from the beginning between the social revolutionary forces which had sprung from the Eastern European masses and the aspiration for national emancipation as formulated by Herzl and his followers in the Central European countries. The paradox of this split was that, whereas the former was actually a people's movement, caused by national oppression, the latter, created by social discrimination, became the political creed of intellectuals.[19]

Lazare constantly urged the 'pariah' Jew to fight the 'parvenu' Jew, who wished to completely forget his Jewish identity through absorption into the affluent society of his hosts.[20] However, Lazare's efforts were not to be rewarded:

> The parvenu who fears lest he becomes a pariah, and the pariah who aspires to become a parvenu, are brothers under the skin and appropriately aware of their kinship. Small wonder,

---

[18] See below.

[19] 'Zionism Reconsidered', in *The Jewish Writings*, p. 348.

[20] 'The Jew as Pariah: A Hidden Tradition', *ibid.*, p. 284.

in face of this fact, that of all Lazare's efforts - unique as they were - to forge the peculiar situation of his people into a vital and significant political factor, nothing now remains.[21]

Nevertheless, even though Arendt favoured socialist aspirations, she grants that Herzl did perform a valuable nationalist service insofar as the assimilation that some Jews enjoyed in the early days of their emancipation did not stand them in good stead when the growing anti-bourgeois sentiments of the Europeans were squarely turned on the Jews by the end of the nineteenth century:

> Yet in considering Herzl's movement as a whole and in assessing his definite merits within the given historical situation, it is necessary to say that Zionism opposed a comparatively sound nationalism to the hidden chauvinism of assimilationism and a relatively sound realism to the obvious utopianism of Jewish radicals.[22]

The Israeli State

Though Arendt supported the creation of an Israeli state and even helped Jews emigrate to Palestine between 1935 and 1939 while she was in exile in France, she did not, as a socialist, approve of many of the state's policies in the early years of its existence. She especially notes the stark difference between the attitude of the assimilated Jews of the nineteenth century to the Jews of the middle of the twentieth. For instance, she notes in her essay 'Jewish Politics' that the situation of young Jews in the 1940s had undergone an alarming transformation:

> The so-called young generation - which ranges in age from twenty to seventy - demands cunning of their politicians but not character, opportunism but not principles, propaganda but not policies. It is a generation that has fallen into the

---

[21] *Ibid.*, p. 286.
[22] 'The Jewish State', in *op. cit.*, p. 381.

habit of constructing its *Weltanschauung* out of a vague trust in great men, out of blood and soil and horoscopes. The politics that grows out of this mentality is called *Realpolitik*. Its central figures are the businessman who winds up being a politician convinced that politics is just a huge oversized business deal with huge oversized wins and losses, and the gangster who declares, "When I hear the word culture I reach for my revolver." Once "abstract" ideas had been replaced by "concrete" stock market speculation, it was easy for abstract justice to give way before concrete revolvers. What looked like a rebellion against all moral values has led to a kind of collective idiocy . . . What looked like a rebellion against intellect has led to organized turpitude – might makes right.[23]

We note here a vivid adumbration of the steady, and fateful, degeneration that Jewry has undergone in the latter part of the twentieth century, especially in its chosen American homeland.

The foundations of the Israeli state

We should, at this point, remember that the state of Israel was the creation of secular Zionists like Herzl who were assimilated western European Jews fearful of anti-Semitic trends in Europe in the latter part of the nineteenth century. They were later supported by the persecuted Jews of eastern Europe, who suffered more acute persecution under the Tsars. Israel was not particularly developed, by either western or eastern Jews, as a religious project. On the other hand, it was – and is still today – opposed on religious grounds by a small group of Orthodox Jews, the Neturei Karta, formed in Palestine in 1938 by Jews from Hungary and Lithuania. Their beliefs are based on Torah dicta regarding the re-establishment of Israel only after the Messiah's return. They believe that the Jews were exiled because of their sins and can be reconstituted as a state only when they are redeemed by the coming of the Messiah.

---

[23] 'Jewish Politics', in *op. cit.*, p. 242

As the Neturei Karta maintain:[24]

> In the past two thousand years of the dangers and sufferings of exile not once did any of the Sages of Israel suggest that we make a state to protect ourselves.

whereas

> The founders of Zionism were all atheists who denied the Torah.

Also, the Israeli state is based on a shaky foundation of artificially fostered anti-Semitism and extorted foreign aid:

> the means by which [the founders of Zionism] planned to establish a state was by instigating anti-Semitism, and undermining the security of the Jews in all the lands of the world, until they would be forced to flee to their state.

> We see that most of world Jewry lives in security and under good physical conditions, and have no desire to go live in the Zionist State. Whereas many people have left the Zionist State to live under better conditions in other lands.

> The Zionist State could not continue to exist without economic support from Jews living outside of the Zionist State.

The group believe that the Israeli state does not represent the Jewish people around and for whom the Biblical texts were composed:

> Zionism will not replace the Jewish People. The Jewish People will remain strong in their faith and the Zionist State will cease to exist.

> It is therefore, our demand that the State that calls itself ISRAEL, should cease to exist.

---

[24] See their website, *Neturei Karta International: Jews united against Zionism* (www.nkusa.org).

The Neturei Karta's reference to the coming of the Messiah as a precondition for the re-establishment of any Israeli state is proven by the case of the Messianic claims of Sabbatai Zevi (1626-76), a Sephardic Jew and Kabbalist from Smyrna (Izmir) who declared himself the Messiah and prophesied the return of the ten tribes of Judah to the Holy Land in 1665. It is interesting to note that Zevi's Messianic claim was made at a time of Jewish persecution in eastern Europe. In 1666, however, he was captured in Constantinople by the Grand Vizier, Ahmed Köprülü, and imprisoned first in Constantinople and then in Abydos. Finally, he was forced to convert to Islam in order to avoid execution at the hands of the Turks.

Socialist and nationalist movements in Israel

The dismantling of the Israeli state called for by the Neturei Karta may at present seem quite unlikely when Israel is solidly protected by its American ally. However, there is another alternative to the present rapacious form of Israel that was first presented in the middle of the twentieth century by the small Ihud party of Palestine, which propagated Arab-Jewish bi-nationalism and was supported by Arendt herself.[25] Ihud was founded in 1946 by Judah Leon Magnes, Martin Buber, Ernst Simon, and Henrietta Szold to foster cooperation between the Zionists and the Arabs. It was allied to the Jewish Labour and Communist parties of Palestine. Magnes originally wished that Jews and Arabs would live peacefully together in Palestine in mostly separate counties or cantons with their own law courts, though there might have been a few mixed counties as well. Jews and Arabs would be represented in equal numbers in the constituent and legislative assemblies.

Magnes believed that by cooperating in government, the Jews and Arabs would cease to consider themselves as mutually

---

[25] See, for instance, 'To Save the Jewish Homeland', in Arendt, *The Jewish Writings*, p. 399.

exclusive residents of Palestine. As he declared in his speech at the 30th United Nations Special Committee on Palestine meeting in Jerusalem in July 1947,

> [w]e propose that Palestine become a bi-national country composed of two equal nationalities, the Jews and the Arabs, a country where each nationality is to have equal political powers, regardless of who is the majority or the minority.[26]

He also wanted Palestine to be a neutral state like Switzerland and the Vatican, lacking an army of its own. Magnes even suggested that Israel should be absorbed into a Semitic federation:

> We think that a bi-national Palestine based on parity has a great mission to help revive this Semitic world materially and spiritually.

For,

> [s]o far as the neighbouring countries are concerned, we believe that the bi-national Palestine based upon parity should become a member in due course of a large federation, a larger union, whether it be the Arab federation or a Union of countries of the Middle East . . . it is perfectly conceivable that some of the other countries of this federation would say, as some have said in days gone by, "We also would like to have some Jewish immigrants in order to help us build our land". That would not mean, of course, that the Jewish National Home would be extended into those countries, but Jewish scientific ability, Jewish organizing power, perhaps finance, perhaps the experience of the West, which many of the countries of this part of the world have need of, might be placed at their disposal for the good of this whole region. In this way reciprocal influence might be felt.

Further, the Ihud party's federative programmes were based on a belief that Jews and Arabs in Palestine might eventually

---

[26] See 'Hearings of representatives from the Ihud (Union) Association – 30th UNSCOP meeting – Verbatim Record', at unispal.un.org

135

belong either to a British commonwealth[27] or to a Mediterranean confederation that would spread across North Africa
and the Levant. Arendt endorsed this plan entirely:

> A further possibility for a reasonable solution of the Palestine
> question would be a kind of Mediterranean federation. In a
> model of this sort the Arabs would be strongly represented
> and yet not in a position to dominate all others. Insofar as it is
> generally recognized that neither Spain, nor Italy, nor France
> can exist economically without their possessions in North
> Africa, this sort of federation would provide for these three
> countries a fair and just solution to the colonial question.
> For Jews it would mean the restoration of both their dignity
> and their place among the nations of the Mediterranean, to
> the cultural glory of which region they have contributed so
> much.[28]

Jews would thus live with Arabs in one state, and in one Arab
and Mediterranean federation. Such a confederation would
certainly benefit the Arabs, who have already absorbed
much European culture in their recent history, as well as the
European Jews. However, the Jews, especially those of the
Jewish Agency, would not consider a future as a minority in
a larger Arab state. By 1947, when the UN had come up with
a Partition Plan, and when in 1948 there followed the War

---

[27] 'There are some of us, if I may make a confession to you, who have
great admiration for the liberalism of Great Britain, for the traditional
liberalism of Great Britain; and, particularly now, if I may speak for
myself: for the way in which Great Britain is trying to change . . . her
Imperialism, which has brought a great deal of unhappiness, into a
Commonwealth; the way she has tried to do it in India, the way she
has tried to do it in Burma, the way she is trying to do it in Egypt,
whether with complete success or not. That is one of the great political
movements of history. That is another reason – if you ask me the
question – why I say Great Britain would probably be the trustee over
this period' (*ibid.*).

[28] 'Between Silence and Speechlessness' in Arendt, *The Jewish Writings*,
p. 197.

of Independence, Ihud's plans for a bi-national state faded from the intellectual and political scene.

Another Palestinian Jewish group that Arendt supported were the Jews who were already resident in Palestine before the establishment of the Israeli state, and who were generally called the *Yishuv* [the People]. Their ideal was mostly that of the construction of an Israeli state through Israeli work, and not through colonialist employment of Palestinian labour. The Kibbutz movement was part of this trend, and belonged to the socialist wing of Israelis who wished to see Israel develop its own indigenous Jewish culture through Jewish efforts. However, the movement remained politically weak and inactive. It also agreed, as Arendt points out, to the Nazi-Zionist transfers during the Third Reich.

As further evidence of the weakness of the Left wing in Jewish Palestine, David Ben-Gurion, who had begun as a leader of the Mapai party, the moderate Zionist labour party, became Chairman of the Executive Committee of the powerful Jewish Agency in 1935, and emphasised the theory of the irreconcilability of Jews and Arabs. He also led the Arab-Israeli War of 1948 and became Israel's first Prime Minister in 1949. During the Six-Day War of 1967, he and General Moshe Dayan occupied the Egyptian Sinai Peninsula, the Syrian Golan Heights, the Jordanian West Bank, and the Egyptian Gaza Strip.

The Revisionist nationalist party, which was established by Ze'ev Jabotinsky in 1923 and was bolstered by the paramilitary Irgun organisation, had a more lasting political life than Zionism's socialist wing. Ben-Gurion himself continuously collaborated with Menachim Begin of the Irgun movement, which was engaged in terrorist attacks, such as the bombing of the King David Hotel in 1946 and the Deir Yassin massacre of Arabs in 1948. During the 1948 war, Ben-Gurion incorporated the Irgun militia into the Israel Defence Forces. The Revisionist Party itself was transformed into the Likud party in 1973, and it rules Israel today. This steady erosion of the socialist aspects of the original Zionist movement is indeed reflected in the relative weakness of the Labour party in Israel ever since the 1995 assassination of the Labour Prime

Minister, Yitzhak Rabin, shortly after his signing of the Oslo Accords with Yasser Arafat.

Lazare and the socialists' revolutionary ambitions thus remained rather idealistic, and were politically ineffective. The Third Reich's anti-Jewish measures had indeed increased pro-Jewish feeling in Palestine and made it more nationalist. The consequence, as Arendt points out, was that Israel began to assume a new 'non-European' character:

> Ideologically more important was the fact that, by their interpretation of Palestine in the future life of the Jewish people, the Zionists shut themselves off from the destiny of the Jews all over the world.[29]

The Zionist idea had now become nationalist in a narrow, quasi-National Socialist sense that worked against the development of the European culture that assimilated Jews had once possessed:

> Among all the misconceptions harbored by the Zionist movement because it had been influenced so strongly by antisemitism, this false notion of the non-European character of the Jews has had probably the most far-reaching and the worst consequences. Not only did the Zionists break the necessary solidarity of European peoples . . . incredibly, they would even deprive the Jews of the only historical and cultural homestead they possibly can have; for Palestine together with the whole Mediterranean basin has always belonged to the European continent: geographically, historically, culturally, if not at all times politically. Thus the Zionists would deprive the Jewish people of its just share in the roots and development of what we generally call Western culture.[30]

Arendt thus came to consider Israel as a capitalist and colonialist – and perhaps also imperialist – state. She feared that such

---

[29] 'Zionism Reconsidered' in *op. cit.*, p. 361.

[30] *Ibid.*, p. 366.

a state could not survive among hostile Arab neighbours.[31] In general, she preferred to focus on the notion of a Jewish home that Jews should be encouraged to fight for, rather than on a Jewish state's constitution. This may be tied to her favourite notion of the 'Jewish pariah', wherein the Jew must live along with others even when feeling himself to be an outsider. She supported Zionism not as a Jewish state, but rather as a Jewish home living in cooperation with the Arabs.

She believed that a socialist state had a greater chance of survival while waiting for the international socialist world. As she outlined in her essay, 'To Save the Jewish homeland' (1948):

1) The real goal of the Jews in Palestine is the building up of a Jewish homeland. This goal must never be sacrificed to the pseudo-sovereignty of a Jewish state.

2) The independence of Palestine can be achieved only on a solid basis of Jewish-Arab cooperation. As long as Jewish and Arab leaders both claim that there is "no bridge" between Jews and Arabs (as Moshe Shertok has just put it), the territory cannot be left to the political wisdom of its own inhabitants.

. . .

5) Local self-government and mixed Jewish-Arab municipal and rural councils, on a small scale and as numerous as possible, are the only realistic political measures that can eventually lead to the political emancipation of Palestine.

She realised that, without cooperation between Arabs and Jews, the constant support of American Jewry would be necessary for Israel's sustenance:

If a Jewish commonwealth is obtained in the near future – with or without partition – it will be due to the political influence of American Jews. This would not need to affect their status of American citizenship if their "homeland," or "mother country," were a politically autonomous entity in a normal

---

[31] Hence her insistence on the need for Israel to develop an army of its own in order to establish its sovereignty.

sense, or if their help were likely to be only temporary. But if the Jewish commonwealth is proclaimed against the will of the Arabs and without the support of the Mediterranean peoples, not only financial help but political support will be necessary for a long time to come. And that may turn out to be very troublesome indeed for Jews in this country, who after all have no power to direct the political destinies of the Near East.[32]

However, already in 1944 she had realised the inevitability of American involvement in the Middle East on account of the oil reserves in the region:

the laying of an oil pipeline from the Persian Gulf to the Mediterranean, as planned by the American government, will become one of the most important factors in postwar politics. Since it has evidently been determined that Arabian oil is to cover much of the needs of European countries, America's future influence on intra-European matters will depend to a large extent on this pipeline.[33]

Furthermore, the Americans clearly use 'the rules of *divide et impera* by which today the Arabs, but possibly tomorrow the Jews, can be assigned the task of guarding oil hubs'.[34]

Nevertheless, the American-Jewish solidarity with Israel was at first relatively slow. Chaim Weizmann, who served as the first President of Israel, called for the return of American Jews to Israel, but they were initially not in favour of such an emigration because they feared accusations of dual loyalty. But the steady drumming-up of support for Israel in America soon succeeded to such an extent that even non-Jewish Americans today consider Israel as their natural partner.

Unfortunately, the victory of the nationalist elements in Israel over the socialists has had disastrous results, not only in the

---

[32] 'Zionism Reconsidered', in *op. cit.*, p. 373.

[33] 'The Political Organization of the Jewish People', *ibid.*, p. 202.

[34] *Ibid.*, p. 203.

Middle East but also in America itself. Herzl's closing words in *The Jewish State*: 'The world will be freed by our liberty, enriched by our wealth, magnified by our greatness',[35] have not been proven by recent history. It is significant in this context that, even though the state of Israel had an oriental Sephardic majority for the first fifty years of its existence, it has increasingly followed Herzl's vision of a state with a majority of European Jews living in a technologically modern land. It is not surprising that the Arabs around the Israeli state are constantly in danger of being dispossessed of their ancestral lands,[36] and that the nations of the world that do not support Israel are thrust into relative poverty as well.

The future of the Jews

We have already noted that, as the Neturei Karta have demonstrated, there is no real religious justification for the establishment of an Israeli state. Besides, Christians – whether American or otherwise – who accept Jesus as the Messiah can never believe in the coming of another Jewish Messiah and can, logically, never accept the creation of a Jewish state that has not become Christian. Herzl's professed reason for it – anti-Semitism in Europe – is also not a major danger any longer. Thus one may believe that it would be better for the Jews to abandon Israel altogether and to live in a continuing diaspora among European host states following the federative plans made by the Ihud party and recommended by Arendt.

If, on the other hand, Israel should be allowed to continue its existence as a political entity, it should, following the socialists, like Arendt, be a Jewish home that is developed by Jews

---

[35] Theodor Herzl, *The Jewish State* (New York: American Zionist Emergency Council, 1946), p. 157.

[36] Indeed, Herzl himself had noted in his private diary that 'the natives of whatever land was allotted to the Jews would be gently persuaded to move to other countries' (see Ami Isseroff, 'Preface' to Herzl, *The Jewish State* at *MidEast Web* [www.mideastweb.org/jewishstate.pdf]).

as a nursery of Jewish culture. That the Jews should turn away from their capitalist preoccupations to more socialist ones is a precondition of their survival in the long run, considering that anti-Semitism was quickened in the nineteenth century mainly by the Jewish capitalist and financial manipulations within Europe's princely states.

If Israel is allowed to continue to exist, it must be included within an Arab and Mediterranean federation that would be allied to the European Union rather than to the United States. It is interesting to recall in this context that the Belgian geopolitical thinker, Jean Thiriart (1922-1992), had also propounded a theory of a united European federation that included Israel as a protectorate. As he stated in a 1987 interview with the American evangelical writer Gene H. Hogberg, Israel must become a protectorate of either Russia or Europe (until these two are united). A united Europe should only tolerate

> a "small" pastoral Israel (with the borders prescribed by the UN), "an Israel of kibbutzes and grapefruit" . . . (while) the Biblical paranoia of the (Israeli) Extreme Right who dream of a Greater Israel stretching to the Euphrates must be denounced and resisted with vigour.[37]

Such an inclusion of Israel as a protectorate into Europe naturally presupposes a break in the intimate political relationship between a nationalist Israel and a Right-wing US, since a European federation such as Thiriart's could certainly not tolerate the anomaly of a pro-American Israel within it. The fact that America has never had a strong socialist factor in its politics means that the only Zionist attitude bolstered by the Americans so far has been an increasingly nationalist Zionist one that provokes the hostility of Israel's neighbours, as well as that of other nations of the world that are either Islamic or in other ways independent of the American-Israeli axis. The Zionist tendencies

---

[37] 'Jean Thiriart: Responses to 14 Questions Submitted by Gene H. Hogberg, Part Four', tr. David Wainwright, at home.alphalink.com. au/~radnat/thiriart/interview4.html.

of the so-called 'Right-wing' parties and governments – as well as of the so-called 'Alt-Right' movement that provides them with an ideological cover – in the US, Europe, and even South America today are a case in point.

Whether a break between Israel and America can actually be accomplished depends partly on the political resurgence of a Europe that is marked by a civilisatory mission such as that envisaged by European nationalists like Thiriart. But it depends also on whether the Israelis themselves are able to live within a tutelary Europe in a socialist rather than a nationalist manner – following Zionists like Lazare, that is, rather than Herzl. If the Jews of the West manage to retain a sense of their peculiar 'pariah' status as Jews – as Varnhagen and Arendt did – and not attempt to distort European culture with American-Jewish vulgarity in the vindictive way that the 'Frankfurt School', for instance, did in the middle of the twentieth century, it is possible that the Jewish Question may yet be resolved in a reasonable manner. The choice that Jews must make between the relatively cultured status of nineteenth-century European Jewry and the 'organised turpitude' of the 'businessmen' and 'gangsters' of twentieth century America is thus a momentous one.

Bibliography

Primary Sources

Adorno, Theodor
Aesthetic Theory, tr. Robert Hullot-Kentor, London-New York: Continuum, 1997.
Prisms, tr. Samuel & Shierry Weber, Cambridge, MA: The MIT Press, 1955.
Philosophy of Modern Music, tr. A. G. Mitchell and W. V. Blomster, New York: The Seabury Press, 1973.
Essays on Music, tr. Susan H. Gillespie, Berkeley-Los Angeles: University of California Press, 2002.

Adorno, Theodor & Horkheimer, Max
Dialektik der Aufklärung: Philosophische Fragmente, Amsterdam: Querido, 1947.
Dialectic of Enlightenment: Philosophical Fragments, tr. Edmund Jephcott, Stanford: Stanford University Press, 2002.

Adorno, Theodor, Frenkel-Brunswik, E., Levinson, D., Sanford, N.
The Authoritarian Personality, New York: Harper and Brothers, 1950.

Arendt, Hannah
The Origins of Totalitarianism, New York: Schocken Books, 1951.
The Human Condition, Chicago, IL: University of Chicago Press, 1958.
On Revolution, NY: Viking Press, 1963.

The Jewish Writings, ed. J. Kohn and R. H. Feldman, New York: Schocken Books, 2007.

Rahel Varnhagen: The Life of a Jewess, tr. R. and C. Winston, Baltimore, MD: Johns Hopkins University Press, 1997.

Burke, Edmund

Reflections on the Revolution in France, in *The Works of Edmund Burke*, Boston: Charles C. Little & James Brown, 1839.

Duchesne, Ricardo

The Uniqueness of Western Civilization, Leiden-Boston: Brill, 2011.

Dühring, Eugen

Die Judenfrage als Racen-, Sitten- und Culturfrage mit einer weltgeschichtlichen Antwort, Karlsuhe: H. Reuther, 1881.

The Jewish Question as a Racial, Moral and Cultural Question, with a World-Historical Answer, London: Ostara Publications, 2017.

Evola, Julius

Gli Uomini e le rovine, Rome: Edizioni dell'Ascia, 1953.

Men among the Ruins, tr. Guido Stucco, Rochester, VT: Inner Traditions, 2002.

Fascism viewed from the Right, tr. E. Christian Kopff, London: Arktos, 2013.

Notes on the Third Reich, tr. E. Christian Kopff, London: Arktos, 2013.

Ferguson, Niall

Civilization: The West and the Rest, New York: Penguin Books, 2011.

Fichte, Johann Gottlieb

The Popular Works of Johann Gottlieb Fichte, tr. W. Smith, London: J. Chapman, 1848.

Addresses to the German Nation, tr. R. F. Jones & G. H. Turnbull, Chicago: Open Court Publishing Co., 1922.

Gentile, Giovanni
Genesis and Structure of Society, tr. H. S. Harris, Urbana, IL: University of Illinois Press, 1946.
'What is Fascism?', in H. W. Schneider, *Making the Fascist State*, New York: Howard Fertig, 1968.
'Fundamental Ideas', in Benito Mussolini, *The Doctrine of Fascism*, tr. I. S. Munro, in *Readings on Fascism and National Socialism*, ed. A. Swallow, Columbus, OH: Swallow Press, 1984.

Hegel, G. W. F.
Lectures on the Philosophy of History, tr. J. Sibree, London: George Bell & Sons, 1881.

Herzl, Theodor
The Jewish State, New York: American Zionist Emergency Council, 1946.

Jung, Edgar Julius
Die Herrschaft der Minderwertigen: The Rule of the Inferiour, 2 vols., tr. Alexander Jacob, Lewiston, NY: Edwin Mellen Press, 1995.

Kojève, Alexandre
Introduction to the Reading of Hegel: Lectures on the Phenomenology of Spirit, ed. Allan Bloom, tr. James Nichols, Jr., New York: Basic Books, 1969.

Kuehnelt-Leddihn, Erik von
The Menace of the Herd, or Procrustes at Large, Milwaukee, WI: Bruce Publishing Co., 1943.
Liberty or Equality: The Challenge of our Time, Caldwell, ID: The Caxton Printers, 1952.

Maistre, Joseph de
On God and Society, tr. E. Greifer, Chicago: H. Regnery Co., 1959

Marr, Wilhelm
Der Sieg des Judenthums über das Germanenthum, Berlin: Rudolph Costenoble, 1879.

Marx, Karl
Ökonomisch-philosophische Manuskripte aus dem Jahre 1844, in K. Marx - F. Engels, *Kleine ökonomische Schriften,* Berlin, 1955.
The Economic and Philosophic Manuscripts of 1844, tr. M. Milligan, Moscow: Progress Publishers, 1959.

Marx, Karl and Engels, Friedrich
Manifest der kommunistischen Partei, London: J. C. Burkhard, 1848.
Manifesto of the Communist Party, tr. S. Moore, 1888.
Das Kapital: Kritik der politischen Oekonomie, 3 vols., Hamburg: Otto Meisner, 1867, 1885, 1894.
Capital: A Critique of Political Economy, tr. S. Moore and E. Aveling, 1887.

Maurras, Charles
'The Future of the Intelligentsia' and 'For a French Awakening', tr. Alexander Jacob, London: Arktos, 2016.

Moeller van den Bruck, Arthur
Das dritte Reich, Berlin: Der Ring, 1923.
Germany's Third Empire, tr. E. O. Lorimer, London: Arktos, 2012.

Scruton, Roger
The Meaning of Conservatism, London: Macmillan, 1984.

Sombart, Werner
Die deutsche Volkswirtschaft im neunzehnten Jahrhundert, Berlin: Georg Bondi, 1903.
Das Proletariat: Bilder und Studien, Frankfurt am Main: Rütten & Loening, 1906.
'Der kapitalistische Unternehmer', in *Archiv für Sozialwissenschaft und Sozialpolitik,* no. 29 (1909).

Die Juden und das Wirtschaftsleben, Leipzig: Duncker und Humblot, 1911.

The Jews and Modern Capitalism, tr. M. Epstein, New York: E. P. Dutton & Co., 1913.

Der Bourgeois: Zur Geistesgeschichte des modernen Wirtschaftsmenschen, Munich: Duncker und Humblot, 1913.

Händler und Helden, Munich: Duncker und Humblot, 1915.

Deutscher Sozialismus, Berlin-Charlottenburg: Buchholz und Weisswange, 1934.

A New Social Philosophy, tr. K. F. Geiser, Princeton, NJ: Princeton University Press, 1937.

Spengler, Oswald

Der Untergang des Abendlandes: Umriss einerMorphologie der Weltgeschichte, 2 vols., 1918-1922.

The Decline of the West, tr. C. F. Atkinson, New York: Alfred A. Knopf, 1926.

Jahre der Entscheidung, Munich: C. H. Beck, 1933.

The Hour of Decision, tr. C. F. Atkinson, London: George Allen and Unwin, 1934.

Preussentum und Sozialismus, Munich: C. F. Beck, 1920.

Selected Essays, tr. D. O. White, Chicago: Henry Regnery Co., 1967.

Syberberg, Hans-Jürgen

Vom Unglück und Glück der deutschen Kunst nach dem letzten Kriege, Munich: Matthes & Seitz, 1990.

On the Fortunes and Misfortunes of Art in Post-War Germany, tr. Alexander Jacob, London: Arktos, 2017.

Thiriart, Jean

'Jean Thiriart: Responses to 14 Questions Submitted by Gene H. Hogberg, Part Four', tr. David Wainwright, at www. home. alphalink.com.au.

Tönnies, Ferdinand
Gemeinschaft und Gesellschaft, Leipzig: Fues Verlag, 1887.

Treitschke, Heinrich von
Politics, vol. I, tr. A. J. Balfour, New York: Macmillan Co., 1916.

Weber, Max
'Die Protestantische Ethik und der Geist des Kapitalismus', in
  Archiv für Sozialwissenschaft und Sozialpolitik, 20 (1904),
  1-54, and 21 (1905), 1-110.
The Protestant Ethic and the Spirit of Capitalism, tr. T. Parsons,
  London: George Allen & Unwin, 1930.
*Wirtschaft und Gesellschaft: Grundriss der verstehenden
  Soziologie*, Tübingen: J. C. B. Mohr, 1921.
On Law and Economy in Society, tr. Max Rheinstein, Cambridge,
  MA: Harvard University Press, 1954.
The Protocols of the Meetings of the Learned Elders of Zion, tr.
  Victor E. Marsden, London: Britons Publishing Society,
  1923.

Secondary Sources

Abraham, Gary
'Max Weber on "Jewish Rationalism" and the Jewish Question', *International Journal of Politics, Culture, and Society*, vol. 1, no. 3 (Spring 1988), pp. 358-391.

Anthony, David W.
The Horse, the Wheel, and Language: How Bronze-Age Riders from the Eurasian Steppes Shaped the Modern World, Princeton: Princeton University Press, 2007.

Bendix, Reinhard
Max Weber: An Intellectual Portrait, Berkeley: University of California Press, 1977.

Furlong, Paul
Social and Political Thought of Julius Evola, London: Routledge, 2011.

Israel, Jonathan I.
Radical Enlightenment: Philosophy and the Making of Modernity, 1650–1750, Oxford: Oxford University Press, 2001.

Jacob, Alexander
Nobilitas: A Study of European Aristocratic Philosophy from Ancient Greece to the Early Twentieth Century, Lanham, MD: University Press of America, 2001.
Ātman: A Reconstruction of the Solar Cosmology of the Indo-Europeans, Hildesheim: Georg Olms, 2005.
Brahman: A Study of the Solar Rituals of the Indo-Europeans, Hildesheim: Georg Olms, 2012.
'The "Dynastic Race" and the Biblical Japheth', Parts I and II, *Ancient Origins* (www.ancient-origins.net), 13-14 Oct. 2017.

Jacob, Margaret
Scientific Culture and the Making of the Industrial West, New York: Oxford University Press, 1997.

Love, John
'Max Weber's Ancient Judaism', in *The Cambridge Companion to Weber*, ed. Stephen Turner, Cambridge: Cambridge University Press, 2000.

Macdonald, Kevin B.
The Culture of Critique: An Evolutionary Analysis of Jewish Involvement in Twentieth Century Intellectual and Political Movements, Westport, CT: Praeger, 1988.

McNeill, William
The Rise of the West: A History of the Human Community, Chicago: University of Chicago Press, 1963.

Mitzman, Arthur
Sociology and Estrangement: Three Sociologists of Imperial Germany, New York: Alfred A. Knopf, 1973.

Murray, Charles
Human Accomplishment: The Pursuit of Excellence in the Arts and Sciences, 800 BC to 1950, New York: HarperCollins, 2003.

Taylor, Charles
Sources of the Self: The Making of the Modern Identity, Cambridge: Cambridge University Press, 1989.

Tilly, Charles
Coercion, Capital, and European States, AD 990-1990, Cambridge, MA: Blackwell, 2002.

Published by Logik Förlag

Albacke, Simon:
Johans tåg, (2019).

Bacu, Dumitru:
The Anti-Humans, (2016).

Berlin, Saga, Jacobson, Mats:
Djuren i Yggdrasil, (2013).
The Animals in Yggdrasil, (2016).
Yggdrasil – Der Weltbaum Und Seine Tiere, (2016).
Les animaux vivant dans Yggdrasil, (2017).

Bjurman, Sebastian:
Flickan som jagades av elden, (2017).

Björkqvist, Björn:
En annan bild av Hitler, (red.), (2005).
Vägvalet, (2014)

Burnham, Stanley:
Svart intelligens i ett vitt samhälle, (2015).

Carlberg, Carl-Ernfrid:
Texter, dikter och bilder, (2012).

Carlqvist, Ingrid:
Från Sverige till Absurdistan, (2018).
Keith och jag, (2017).

Chamberlain, Houston Stewart:
Demokrati och frihet, (2015).
Politiska ideal, (2017).

Codreanu, Corneliu Z.:
Fängelsedagbok, (2017).
Till mina legionärer, (2007).
The Prison Notes, (2015).

Dahlberg, Per:
Den nordiska ledartanken, (2006).

Degrelle, Léon:
Epos, (2006).
Fälttåget på östfronten, (2012, 2016).

Dixon Jr., Thomas:
Vita ryttare, (2015).
Duke, David:
Den judiska rasismen, (2015).
Kämpa för nordisk frihet, (2013).
Mitt uppvaknande, (2015).
Eckehart, Meister:
Hur Sverige blev en mångkultur, (2007).
How Sweden Became Multicultural, (2017).
Eriksson, Sven:
Mod och trohet, pliktuppfyllelse och kamratskap, (2015).
Samhällets väl före egennytta: Tysk socialpolitik 1933-1940, (2017).
Ewers, Hanns Heinz:
Horst Wessel: En biografi, (2018).
Faurisson, Robert:
Mitt liv som revisionist, (2007).
Revisionismens segrar, (2008).
Flodæus, Olof:
Röd död, (2012).
Garfvé, Henrik:
Ras och IQ, (2006).
Guénon Réne:
Kvantitetens herravälde och tidens tecken, (2019).
Göring, Hermann:
Tyskland återfött, (2015).
Hageback, Niklas:
Idiots breed Idiots, (2018).
Idioter föder idioter, (2018).
Hansson, Per:
Demokratin som dödgrävare, (2012).
Harwood, Richard:
Nürnbergprocessen, (2008).
Holland, Derek:
Den politiske soldaten, (2017).

Johnson, Greg:
Det nationalistiska manifestet, (2019)
Nya högern kontra gamla högern, (2015).
Sanning, rättvisa och ett trevligt vitt land, (2016)
Kemp, Arthur:
Jihad, (2016).
Kjellén, Rudolf:
Nationalitetsidén, (2009).
Nationell samling, (2016).
Kjellman, Östen:
Tankar i skogen, (2013).
Unghögern, (2015, 2018).
Vilka började andra världskriget?, (2013).
Knudsen, Harald Franklin:
I was Quisling's Secretary, (2017).
Jag var Quislings sekreterare, (2016).
Kruger, Paul:
Settlement of the Boer-Afrikaner People's Claim to
territorial self-determination, (2018).
Lamb, Lash John:
Inte i herrens avbild, (2019).
Le Bon, Gustave:
Massans psykologi, (2016).
Lindholm, Sven Olov:
Svensk frihetskamp, (2012).
Macdonald, Andrew:
Jägaren, (2012).
Turners dagböcker, (2009).
MacDonald, Kevin:
Att förstå det judiska inflytandet, (2012).
Västerlandet och dess fiender, (2015).
Malynski, E., de Poncins, L., Evola, J.:
The Occult War, (2015).
Molin, Adrian:
Stafetten går vidare, (2016).
Svenska spörsmål och krav, (2017).

Nilsson, Anders:
Wotans Väg: Asatro och det nordiska själskomplexet, (2020).
Nilsson, Jonas:
Anarko-fascism: Naturen återfödd, (2017).
Anarcho-fascism: Nature Reborn, (2017).
När migration blir konflikt, (2019)
Nilsson, Jonas & Stigermark, Anton (Red.):
Att förstå alternativhögern, (2017).
Nordengruppen:
Ett annat Tyskland, (2011).
Olfwenstam, Jan-Eric C.:
Dold spindel, (2017).
Oredsson, Vera:
När flaggstängerna blommade, (2016).
When the Flagpoles Bloomed, (2018).
Notizie Provita:
The Attack on the Family, (2019).
Rami, Ahmed:
Tabubelagda tankar, (2005).
Rosberg, Johan Evert:
Nordiskt kynne: Jämförande karakteristiker, (2017).
Rushton, J. Philippe:
Ras, evolution och beteende, (2014).
Sennels, Nicolai:
Helig vrede: Bland kriminella muslimer, (2017).
Holy Wrath: Among Criminal Muslims, (2018).
Snellman, Juha:
Slavarnas tidsålder, (2016).
Slavarnas tidsålder II: Gökinvasion, (2018).
Trasiga liv och bristande bot, (2017).
Stigermark, Anton:
Memetisk krigföring, (2018).
Sundbärg, Gustav:
Det svenska folklynnet, (2016).
Svensson, Lennart:
Burning Magnesium, (2018).
Ett rike utan like: Sveriges historia, (2017).
Trotylstorm i öster, (2018).

Söderman, Magnus:
Den trotsiga, (2013).
Glimtar av liv, (2019)
Odalfolket och mannaförbunden, (2018)
Till värn för Norden, (2011).
Tørning, Kristian:
Egohumanisterna: De nya totalitärerna, (2018).
The Ego Humanists: The new totalitarians (2019)
Ulmnäs, Tommy:
Sverige: Från välfärdsstat till fattigland, (2018).
Waerland, Are:
Känn dig själv: En studie av den svenska folkkaraktären, (2017).
Windeskog, Jimmy:
Under blodröda fanor, (2016).

Lightning Source UK Ltd.
Milton Keynes UK
UKHW040917060323
418105UK00005B/740